kamera
BOOKS

kamerabooks.com

James Clarke

THE FILMS OF PIXAR ANIMATION STUDIO

kamera
BOOKS

First published in 2013 by Kamera Books
an imprint of Oldcastle Books,
PO Box 394, Harpenden, Herts, AL5 1XJ
kamerabooks.com

A CIP catalogue record for this book is available from the British Library.

ISBN
978-1-84243-937-1
978-1-84243-938-8 (epub)
978-1-84243-939-5 (kindle)
978-1-84243-940-1 (pdf)

2 4 6 8 10 9 7 5 3 1

Typeset by Elsa Mathern in Univers 9 pt
Printed and bound by CPI Group (UK) Ltd, Croydon, CR0 4YY

For David Groves and happy memories of talking movies under Warwick University skies.

ACKNOWLEDGEMENTS

Thanks so much to Hannah Patterson for agreeing to bring this idea for a book to life and also my thanks to David Jones, Ashley Nunn and Rick Goldsmith. And, finally, thank you to Anne Hudson, my editor, for bringing everything together.

For me, a feature animated film has to have something besides comedy in order for the audience to stay with it and get everything else it has to offer.

– Brad Bird[1]

The pseudo-information of fiction poses an evolutionary puzzle: why do we not prefer only true information? [...] A work of art acts like a playground for the mind, a swing or a slide or a merry-go-round of visual or aural or social pattern.

– Brian Boyd[2]

Character animation, as opposed to other forms of animation, was built around a vaudeville vocabulary, and remains a graphic trapeze act even today.

– Norman Klein[3]

It is this sense of wondrous change... that distinguishes the literary fairy tale from the moral story, novella, sentimental tale, and other modern short literary genres.

– Jack Zipes[4]

If a movie is good... it sucks you into this dream world.

– Randy Thom[5]

CONTENTS

INTRODUCTION

FROM OBSCURITY TO BEYOND

If you look sharply, when watching *Toy Story 3*, you'll catch a fleeting shot that occurs about midway through the film's running time. The shot is an image of a bee stitched into the rucksack that's carried by a little girl named Molly. But wait! But why? Because this isn't just an ordinary, generic bee. Rather, it's an image of a very particular critter whose name is Wally B. Okay; but why should we be so attentive to this 'beeish' detail? Well, it's because Wally B is no less than the star of Pixar's first ever short film, *The Adventures of Andre and Wally B*, which was first screened in 1984. The film, which was not attached to a feature release, had a very low-key premiere and there's a reference to the event in issue 26 of the subscription publication *Bantha Tracks* (which was published quarterly by Lucasfilm to promote its movies between 1978 and 1987), where we read the following notice: 'On Friday August 31st (1984), Ed Catmull from the Computer Graphics division of Lucasfilm, presented (at Lucasfilm) a computer animated film entitled *The Adventures of Andre and Wally B* which displayed the latest in computer graphics techniques.'[6]

How many viewers of Pixar's subsequent films would know about this relatively quiet corner of modern animation history? Relatively speaking? Well, 'not many' is probably the correct answer. This fleeting moment of intertextuality, then, reminds us of the now extensive and familiar story-world that Pixar has established over a quarter of a century. The studio's output, which also encompasses short-film production as well as its core business of feature-film projects, has become a wellspring that the studio is able to refer to, and draw from, in the knowledge that quite a number of fans will easily make the intertextual connections. The unassuming Wally B cameo is a cute one for sure, evidencing the producers' awareness that there are enough keen-eyed Pixar viewers out there who will enjoy noticing the reference to its earliest fantasy.

Under a starry Parisian sky a rat doubts the value and wisdom of his decision to leave the quiet of life on the farm for the noise of the city. It's a muted moment in a busy, dynamic and energetic film entitled *Ratatouille* (2007). As in real life, though, it's in these quiet, fleeting moments that the most affecting instances of 'reel' life are often to be found, and it seems that animation can render such incidents with the particular subtlety and recognisable human sensibility that give authenticity to the ultra-artificial world of the computer-animated film. No matter how much technological wonder is applied, it's the way in which the human soul is being expressed that we're really connecting with.

ANIMATION AND A PHILOSOPHICAL MOMENT

It's fair to say that you never know when you're going to encounter a bright idea, and that's as true for the folks who tell the stories as it is for those who watch or read their work.

One of the fascinations of the Pixar Animation studio is how consistently it has animated a particular bright idea which, in fairness, probably seems extremely remote from the popcorn of the multiplex or the realm of the movie-download website where you first saw one of the studio's films. What am I talking about?

Well, it's this: Pixar has shown itself to be steeped in the great tradition of American romanticism and, more particularly, in the focus on self-development that emerged during the nineteenth century in North America.

But what is American romanticism, anyway? After all, we're just talking about a cartoon here. But that's precisely it. One of the wonders of animation is that, whilst we're being blissfully entertained and distracted, we're also being presented with a very specific way of looking at the world.

Before we go any further, then, we had best find ourselves a useful definition of American romanticism. From the brief, easy-to-grasp summary I'll offer here I think it's fair to say that you can see the connection to Woody, Remy, Marlin, Russell and other characters in the Pixar story-world. More generally, romanticism can be thought of as an attitude to life and an expression of how it functions (in other words, relationships between people). Critically, it's an outlook that is a deeply embedded part of the popular American film. In the *Oxford Companion to United States History* (edited by Paul S Boyer) we're given the following definition: 'American romanticism – transcendentalism – pantheism, consciousness to the external world, symbolism in nature and literature, self-development. The Victorian era emphasised self-development and the *bildungsroman* came out of that.'[7]

Bildungsroman: it's the German word for a narrative that charts the spiritual and intellectual growth of a main character. This coming-of-age sensibility certainly informs much of the Pixar storytelling mode. Having very briefly dipped our toe in these more philosophical waters (an opportunity never to be shunned) let's turn our attention to images and, in the first instance, to the still images that have been generated as a part of Pixar's conceptual development for each of its films.

If you look at the widely available breadth of illustrated material generated in the development of each Pixar film you'll conclude, I think, that much of this material, created in service of eventual moving pictures, has the quality of picture-book illustrations. Certainly, the tradition of illustration is an ancient art that reaches back to the people of earliest human history, recording and embellishing their experience and imaginings. Joseph Campbell has written of these earliest illustrations that 'the pictures on the rocky walls are never at the entrances (of caves) but begin where the light of day is lost and unfold, then, deep within.'[8] As a description of something so very ancient, it also sounds as though it's referring to something familiarly modern.

Key to Pixar's visual sensibility is the studio's creative inheritance of the work of various popular visual artists, notably the American illustrator Norman Rockwell. Rockwell worked right in the heart of the twentieth century, often referred to as the 'American Century', when American industry and culture dominated the western world. Certainly, a part of this cultural influence came from the popular American movies that exposed large numbers of people to particular American values and narratives. Of Rockwell's work, much has been written, and it has become a widely known touchstone for many people. His paintings offered his audience a typically romanticised and sentimental perspective on subjects such as childhood and iconic figures recognisable in many communities. Rockwell could also hit harder with his work, notably in a painting such as *The Problem We All Live With*, or in the sombre, but stirring, series of images entitled *The Four Freedoms*. It's reasonable to think, then, that Pixar has a healthy working knowledge and understanding of what Rockwell's images achieved as images communicating ideas. The two elements are intertwined and inseparable. In the book *Norman Rockwell: Pictures for the American People*, Thomas Hoving writes that: 'As America moved forward with its twentieth century agenda it also looked backward drawing on the past to justify its newfound world leadership. Rockwell's pictures played a role in shaping this sense of the past...'[9]

Extending the connection between Rockwell's images and Pixar's visual identity, a key point to make is about Pixar's interest in photorealism and the studio's use of many live-action aesthetic techniques, such as the use of shallow focus, whereby foreground characters are placed in focus and the background is indistinct, thereby allowing the audience to concentrate on the characters above all else at a given moment. The question could be asked, though:

why make an animated film if you're going to mimic the devices of live action so extensively? Clearly such concerns don't prevent too many people from immersing themselves in the Pixar movie-world.

If you are one of those people who find themselves eternally romanced by movies in all of their varieties of scope and scale, style and subject, then there's that satisfying moment when you look afresh at the collected work of a director, a producer, a screenwriter, an actor, or perhaps even a studio (from the majors to some smaller outfit for whom you feel a real enthusiasm), and realise how consistently and vividly achieved their productions have been. The achievement might be all the more admirable given the commercial imperatives that underpin popular moviemaking. The movies that you watch repeatedly become worlds unto themselves, entirely self-contained in their artifice yet entirely in rhyme with how we can really feel and think. When you have that moment with a movie (and it happens just as easily with the worlds of literature, music, sport, computer gaming), seeing how it echoes and perhaps enriches the vision of how you would like the world to be, it's an epiphany that you never forget. The wish fulfilment that's a part of this experience is key to the popular film.

Animation historian and scholar Maureen Furniss has made a useful observation about a spectrum on which all animated films sit. At one end of the line is animation that mimics reality, whilst at the other we have animated projects that move increasingly towards abstraction and anti-realism of visual forms, plot patterns, character design, and use of sound.

Since its breakout moment in late 1995 with the feature film *Toy Story*, Pixar Animation Studio's films have been immensely popular, establishing themselves as stories that audiences have found entertaining and resonant enough for many return visits. I'm sure a lot of us can think of how often young children will repeatedly watch, within a short timeframe, a film they enjoy. Someone in my family enjoys nothing more than going for 'some peace and quiet' –

which means reclining on the sofa, laptop in place, with the Disney adaptation of *Beauty and the Beast* playing for the zillionth time. Pixar's films, in keeping with the tradition of many Hollywood films, are both a great escape from, and great connection to, reality. It's been documented enough elsewhere how a sense of realism is crucial to the aesthetic of the American popular animated feature. Have a look at the language of this press release announcing new Pixar-produced software. The press release is dated 20 January 2012 and is to promote Pixar's latest iteration of its proprietary RenderMan software: 'For two decades Pixar's Academy Award-winning RenderMan has led the revolution in rendering visual effects and animation, and is the standard for creating the outstanding levels of visual photorealism that audiences expect.'[10] The importance of realism to the Pixar film also resides in how it builds its drama and comedy around characters possessed of some believable psychology that's rooted in cause and effect. Their characters are precisely that because they are more than just groovy visual designs, and surely it's this human element that contributes so much to the studio's commercial success.

WHY ANIMATE A STORY?

It's a long way from a Pixar movie, but let's start by quoting a useful insight about storytelling that's been offered up by the American novelist (and occasional screenwriter) Paul Auster, who has written very nicely about film in his novels *The Book of Illusions* and *Man in the Dark*. Auster has observed that, 'This is the power of story: it's irreducible. It's the things that we can't make full sense of that stay with us.'[11] This 'irreducible quality' plays its part in the way that Pixar's films stay with their audiences beyond that first viewing. Putting it most simply: the films have the ring of truth about them. But why might this be? Beyond their surface charms, what are the qualities that make Pixar's stories replay so readily in our memories and prompt us to watch them perhaps more than once or twice, whether by intent or because we catch one of them as we channel surf, only to then find that the task we were about to take care of has been rather delayed due to our sitting perched on the edge of the chair, watching the film until its conclusion.

Before we explore further the storytelling dynamics and allure of Pixar's work, however, we need to go way, way back into the relative pre-history of it all, to a statement made by a late, great cultural icon, about the world of computing and digital realities.

Here is that statement:

Image computing will explode during the next few years.[12]

These nine words were spoken by the late Steve Jobs, and they are quoted in a press release dated 3 February 1986. And the occasion of the press release? Well, it was this: for $5,000,000, Steve had recently bought from George (Lucas) what would soon afterwards be named Pixar. Jobs then put up an additional $5,000,000 to fund the nascent company that he now owned. Also quoted in this landmark press release was Ed Catmull who had been working at Lucasfilm in its Computer Graphics division when Jobs bought it up. Talking about computer imaging processing power, Catmull prophetically anticipated our current digital knowledge age commenting that, 'Society's ability to generate large amounts of data far exceeds its ability to assimilate this data.'[13]

These large amounts of data have indeed been assimilated and manipulated in the service of the creation of virtual shapes, colours and movements that have significantly contributed to pushing the pop culture punch of animation to great success, in doing so reminding us of the immense history of creative human visual endeavour. We've put a lot of time and energy and resources into making up stories across the last many thousands of years. It's a history that begins with the paintings our ancestors made on cave and rock walls and it extends through to visually appealing apps on our smartphones.

In *Film Comment* magazine, a brief piece recently parsed the Pixar identity and made the point that, 'I doubt that Jobs knew just how explosive the growth of animation would prove to be. From

1989 to 1993, the genre had accounted for less than three per cent of the domestic box office, and 90 per cent of that total was Disney. Thanks to Pixar's lead, with DreamWorks Animation following in its wake, animation accounted for nearly 15 per cent of total US and Canadian box office from 2007 to the end of November of 2011.'[14]

THE ROAD TO PIXAR

Boldness of technique, then, was arguably a key characteristic of the initial, primordial version of what would become Pixar; a studio that has sought to apply emerging technologies to established animation and illustration aesthetics and cinematic storytelling in terms of revealing character, presenting action, and maximising the opportunities found in movies for moving between a wide shot and a close-up. Cinematic storytelling is also about what you don't show. Absence makes the audience's heart grow fonder for the pieces of a story to be slotted together. Narrative cinema, in terms of characters, tends to encourage the audience to focus on a character who we want to see succeed and overcome obstacles; the very condition that characterises the experience of life that we all share. Stories are our lives, and our lives are stories.

Forty-one years ago, in 1972, at the University of Utah, two young computer scientists named Ed Catmull and Fred Parker worked on what was to become a watershed in filmmaking and, more specifically, in the animation realm. In the history of computer graphic imaging it's a moment analogous perhaps with the eventual realisation of how to 'realistically' render perspective in painting during the Renaissance. Or perhaps it's up there with Orville and Wilbur Wrights's adventures in flight.

At the University of Utah, Catmull and Parker had constructed an image of a digital hand and animated it in simple but compelling ways so that a finger was flexed. This important test film is available to view online and it takes you through the process that Catmull and Parker undertook to realise the 'illusion'. First, a clay model of Catmull's left hand was made and then marked up into polygons drawn directly onto the clay model. These polygons of intersecting lines were then scanned into the computer, thereby creating a 'mesh' version of the hand constructed from the lines of the intersecting polygons. It is the earliest rendered 3D animation and the short film presents this realisation as well as including images of a digitally rendered human face. It indicates, too, the possibility of applying the technology and new creativity to the realm of medicine.

As with all evolutionary processes, one connection leads to another and finally to an emerging sense of quicksilver transformation and sophistication. Suffice to say, several years after the Utah break-through, another watershed was reached... although this time not by Catmull and Parker.

In 1979, at the SIGGRAPH (Special Interest Group Graphics) conference, a young computer scientist named Loren Carpenter presented *Vol Libre*, a short film that he had made entirely using computer software. Its significance lay in it being the first fractal movie in which a virtual camera presented the illusion of apparently moving over a realistic-looking, virtual landscape. Ed Catmull, in his capacity as a Lucasfilm delegate, was so intrigued by *Vol Libre* that he immediately offered Carpenter a job, and Carpenter's 'film' (graphic sequence) soon became the germ for the way in which the Genesis effect of a planet being born was shown in *Star Trek II: The Wrath of Khan* (Nicholas Meyer, 1982), one of ILM's earliest non-Lucas-produced feature film commissions, which was a watershed moment in the evolution of computer-generated activity in a movie. This film, shortly followed by the release of the technologically pioneering *Tron* (Steven Lisberger, 1982), *Return of the Jedi* (Richard Marquand, 1983) and the lesser-known *The Last Starfighter* (Nick Castle, 1984), began to evidence the emergence and gathering critical mass of computer-generated (CG) images within the broader context of live-action filmmaking. CG, though, was a very expensive form of illusion-making and it would take another ten years before computer-generated (human-generated, really; we never actually say 'paintbrush-generated' paintings, do we?) characters, objects and settings achieved true creative legitimacy and economic viability for film producers. It goes without saying that 25 years is an epoch in computer technology timescales and, hence, what was ultra-sophisticated then is now readily available for application on your home computer or even your smartphone.

Begun as a computer hardware and software research department at Lucasfilm in northern California in the early 1980s, Pixar emerged out of filmmaker George Lucas's special-effects needs. When Lucas realised that, in terms of business practice, he had no need for the company any longer as ILM was expanding and itself working with digital image making, he sold Pixar to Steve Jobs. Of Pixar's origin point at Lucasfilm, Ed Catmull has said, 'Ultimately, the various high technology applications of our work diverged from basis filmmaking.'[15]

Fascinatingly, cultural history is strewn with myriad examples of a group of creatives coming together at a certain place and point in time to work together and inform each other's endeavours. In retrospect, these may look like prophetic moments, but at the time, no doubt, they seemed like just another day. Only now, with the narrative of history threading through and organising our individual and collective memories, can the embellishments of storytelling transform a reality we could only have really known had we been there. This sense of a key moment of like minds converging certainly has a place in the Pixar pre-history.

The time: the 1970s. The place: the Disney animation studio in Los Angeles and also CalArts (established in 1961 by Walt Disney for training prospective animator employees). Amongst the students present in the class of 1977 were John Lasseter and another aspiring animator named Tim Burton, John Musker, who went on to be an animation director at Disney, and Brad Bird, who would go on to work on the Spielberg-produced *Amazing Stories* (1985) and *Batteries Not Included* (Matthew Robbins, 1987) before venturing into *The Simpsons* and subsequently directing the fabulous animated feature *The Iron Giant* (1999).

After graduating from CalArts, John Lasseter worked at the Disney studio on films such as *The Fox and the Hound* (Ted Berman and

Richard Rich, 1981) and *Mickey's Christmas Carol* (Bunny Mattinson, 1983). As has been well chronicled elsewhere, the Disney studio at the time was experiencing a commercially difficult period as it sought to adjust to the movie-taste climate of the late 1970s and early 1980s; a commercial climate in which the prevailing elements were really characterised by the films produced by Steven Spielberg and George Lucas. During this time, Lasseter began imagining what route animation might next take in the final decades of the twentieth century. After all, animation had been a fundamental origin point for cinema.

Lasseter worked as an animator on the TV film *Mickey's Christmas Carol* (1983). Concurrently, for a period of time, in another part of the Disney studio, other animators were working on *Tron* (Steven Lisberger, 1982). Intrigued by the possibilities that might exist in fusing 'classical', hand-drawn animation with the toolset provided by computers, Lasseter wanted to explore further. In 1982, Tron had been released and marked a significant moment in terms of the computer-generated image aesthetic. This was the same year in which *Star Trek II: The Wrath of Khan* (Nicholas Meyer, 1982) came out, featuring the Genesis effect. A pencil and paper, like a computer and a movie camera, are technology. Each of these tools can be used to make tangible the numinous wonders of ideas and emotions. Why not throw them together and see what creatively combusts?

And so, in the early 1980s, Lasseter was able to create, in collaboration with Glen Keane, a short, test-case film (adapting a moment from Maurice Sendak's book *Where the Wild Things Are*; a title that was eventually realised as a terrific live-action film directed by Spike Jonze that was steeped in melancholy) that explored the potential in the fusion of 'traditional' hand-drawn animation with the potential of computer animation. The proof of concept was produced using MAGI Synthavision.

The test footage begins with a close-up of the word 'Max' being written on the wall by Max. The camera pulls back to reveal Max in his familiar 'wild thing' outfit from the book. We see his bedroom in its entirety and the camera is high up. His dog then bounds in and Max jumps onto him, and the dog takes cover under the bed, and the camera drops down, and then Max chases the dog out of the room, with the camera tracking the characters as they run downstairs before moving ahead of them and sweeping across the floor. There's a fluidity to the sequence that anticipates the energy of Pixar's films. The bedroom setting even suggests the *Toy Story* films. It's telling and pertinent, I think, that what they chose to adapt was the work of the late Maurice Sendak. As a writer and illustrator, Sendak has, arguably, become critical to the broader aesthetic sensibility of Pixar. *Monsters, Inc* (Peter Docter, 2001) might most readily come to mind but, more generally, there is that Sendakian sense of the real world housing other wonders. The work of children's book authors Chris Van Allsburg and Dr Seuss also offers us an interesting context in which to consider Pixar's films. No movie is made in a creative vacuum and the echoes of traditions and evolutions find a voice in the next thing that is made.

Lasseter's choice to test drive new technology by adapting Sendak's picture book anticipates a now well-established Pixar narrative format in which a boy's (or man-child's) sense of his horizons is profoundly changed by the end of a larger-than-life adventure. In essence, this resembles each of Pixar's movie narratives. It's an experience that makes sense to all of us, whether we've been adventuring in fantasy realms or not.

Ed Catmull had led the effort at Pixar during its time as a part of Lucasfilm, and he had become, and remains, central to its wider, strategic 'big picture'. The studio began by producing animated content for television commercials, selling products like Listerine and Tropicana, and soon became recognised for its animated short productions, such as *Tin Toy* and *Knick Knack*. In 1990, the Pixar image computer hardware was sold off, allowing the company to focus its energies on animation and software development. By 1993, Pixar had 80 employees and a quickly galvanising capacity to consider a long-form, computer-animated project. Pixar was gaining critical mass.

For some, though, computer animation's development since 1995 – if we treat that year, which saw the release of *Toy Story*, as a watershed for the feature film industry's commitment to computer animation – has not evolved the same subtleties as hand-drawn animation did in a shorter timeframe in the early twentieth century. Here's animation scholar and historian Michael Barrier writing for the *Huffington Post*: 'When you think about how Disney went from *Steamboat Willie* in 1928 to *Snow White* less than ten years later, I think it's extremely compressed (growth) that I don't think computer animation has really approached. What you have instead in computer animation is a continuing elaboration on texture and surfaces and three dimensional space without anything comparable for the characters.'[16]

Animation, then, is rich with examples that wilfully and brilliantly run counter to the realist aesthetic, instead sharpening our delight in the power of metaphor, of free association, of imagination. You've only to watch a film such as *The Monk and the Fish* (Michael Dudok de Wit, 1994), *The Hand* (Jiri Trnka, 1965) or *Neighbours* (Norman McLaren, 1952). We might say that imagination frequently comes to our emotional rescue and that animated films offer a particularly resonant route to this experience.

Understanding and recognising the achievements of animation, therefore, might just be enhanced by engaging with an awareness about certain rules of visual design and aesthetics that can be identified in the movie we're watching. By extension, we can ask the question, 'Is the animated film the most cinematic kind of film?' After all, animation can 'only' exist as a film. That's where its reality is, and it is perhaps the case in terms of computer-animated films that are generated entirely using software (1s and 0s). Of the mystery inherent in a digital system being used by humans in such a way as to conjure the illusion of the mechanised quality of film, John Lasseter (Pixar's first director and now creative lead) has said, 'That's why Pixar films have always had this movie feeling about them. For instance, we invented motion blur for computer animation. The way that a 35mm camera works is that it has a disc that spins – its 180-degree shutter.

Half of that disc is clear, and half is solid. As it spins, half of the time it's exposing the frame, and the frame is still. And when the disc is blank is when the frame advances, and it holds there and is exposed. So there is a look that 35mm has in the way that it blurs, because of this framing. So we studied that and we modelled that into our system when we created motion blur, to get that same look. This was on the first short I created in 1984, *The Adventures of André and Wally B*. It looked so real, even to myself. But it's not real because our eyes don't see motion blur. It's a limitation of the [film camera's] lens. This understanding of the limitations of how films are actually made, and then modelling that within the computer, is classic Pixar. In live action, you get that for free, but we had to create it.'[17]

To put it another way: you can't go out and see the 'real' Woody and Buzz, for example, on the street. The wire-frame character only exists as such in the machine. Indeed, to borrow a phrase, we could say that computer animation offers us the ghost in the machine.

It's understandably easy to be romanced by the technology and capacities of computer imaging, just as it is by many other technologies that conjure illusion. We can also be romanced by the technique of storytelling traditions, by the varied architectures and shifts of tone, relevance and resonance in a given story. Might stories in fact be the ultimate software? Certainly, the oldest of stories productively manage to reboot themselves across hundreds, or even thousands, of years, and these more ancient tales possess a tangible power that's rooted in speech, song, dance and images: the very DNA for motion pictures, we might say. 'Both vaudeville and the cartoon engage the pandemonium of the industrial takeoff after 1870 in Europe and America, when mass culture began a schizoid process: rural nostalgia pitted against the man-made, urban culture.'[18]

In his book *The Origin of Stories*, Brian Boyd considers many subjects, including the work of Dr Seuss (the pen name of Theodor Geisel) and what Boyd observes is, I think, very applicable to Pixar's work. He writes that, 'Dr Seuss faced a number of recurrent problems in each of his books. He wished to appeal to children and their parents, to first time readers and rereaders. He made his stories as much like play as possible, yet as artful as possible, saturating them with the cognitive toying with pattern that underlies all art. [...] And from the first he tries to maximise the benefits of attention and minimise the costs of concentration.'[19] This idea of stories and play comes through in Pixar's movies and, more broadly, across the form of animation. It's also worth noting that animation is not a genre and never has been. A genre is a set of narrative patterns and character types and ideologies. Interestingly, the popular American film's tendency towards playfulness has meant that, generally, it gets mistaken for distraction and disengagement with 'reality', but often it has proved quite the opposite. Think, too, about how readily a great number of animated characters have come to exist beyond the stories in which they were originally introduced to audiences. We recognise these characters outside of their storyworlds. Of the grand tradition of the American animated film, animation scholar Paul Wells has written that, 'Against all the odds, animated film remains the ultimate survivor because it adapts best to technological developments, economic difficulty and creative opportunity. The situation is always difficult but animation can work in so many ways, and speak to so many disciplines and visual "needs" it remains the most flexible and progressive form of expression'.[20] Intriguingly, then, certain animated characters have become like little gods or talismans. These characters embody values and attitudes that hold emotional appeal for us as well as simply looking just plain cool and intriguing. For many people, Mickey Mouse does not exist as a movie star any longer but, instead, as a logo and as a character in a computer game (*Epic Mickey*), as the star of a TV series for preschool children, and as a cuddly toy.

At its best we might say that an animated film (of any type, and telling a story set in any genre) restores our sense of how vividly cinema can imagine events rather than merely being a record of 'characters' speaking to each other. Indeed, if we're lucky, the apparent pursuit of visual realism that's seen in so much cinema as the apogee of creativity might get a run for its money in the world of animation. As scholar Norman Klein notes, 'Cartoons always adjust their graphics to the audience perception of the time.'[21]

Indeed, to put Pixar's work within the broader span of American studio animation, it's worth noting here how the studio connects back to the tradition of the Disney studio, where they developed characterisation in their feature-film adaptations of fairy tales by combining the characters on offer in the source material with the example of nineteenth-century melodramatic characterisation that influenced so heavily the evolution of popular American cinema in the early twentieth century.

Intriguingly, for each Pixar movie (feature or short) there's a developmental process at work that's based around the creation of sketches rendered using pencil, charcoal, pastel sketches and coloured paintings. Models of characters and environments are made, and, ultimately, the images that comprise the completed film, which have the illusion of having been photographed, have been built solely by software and hardware in a virtual context. The computer, then, provides the final iteration of the sketches: just look at how closely the first marker-pen sketch of Mike and Sulley from *Monsters, Inc* resembles their eventual appearance in the movie.

PIXAR FIXATED

Rather like an attachment one may feel to a sports team, the same is true of the attachment that we can feel towards a particular film or filmmaker. Certainly, any time that a Pixar movie is released, there's understandably, and necessarily for the studio, a significant amount of media coverage in the weeks surrounding the release as a major part of the promotional activity. This little book attempts to move past those first impressions and constructions based on original reviews and the necessities of marketing 'hype'. What I want to try and do here is explore how the films resonate with audiences, shot for shot, scene for scene, sequence for sequence. If we can pay attention to specifics rather than generalisations, that might be a good thing.

It's worth observing that Pixar belongs to a fascinating and longstanding tradition which is that of the American inventor, Benjamin Franklin, who even became the focus of the Disney produced animated short *Ben and Me* (1953), is an early example of such a fascinating iconic figure. Franklin said of invention (and let's take this to refer to ideas as well as devices, though of course an idea is a device, too, in many ways) that 'an investment in knowledge always pays the best interest'.[22]

The almost mythic status occupied by the American inventor, and their inventor 'spirit', is compelling to many, and we can readily name Walt Disney, Bill Gates and Steve Jobs as modern and contemporary emblems of this national fascination. As Arthur C Clarke commented, 'Any sufficiently advanced technology is indistinguishable from magic.'[23]

The Russian filmmaker Sergei Eisenstein was a Disney fan who explained that what he responded to in Walt's productions was the way he created 'on the conceptual level of man not yet shackled by logic, reason or experience'.[24] This interest in something youthful and somehow fantastical echoes a little the idea of the 'colours of fantasy' that the German writer Goethe considered in his work 'Reflection in Art and in Colour'.[25]

Eisenstein's implication that there is something interesting about the everyman, the common man, also connects to the work of the scholar Scott McCloud, who Maureen Furniss quotes as saying in his book, *Understanding Comics*, that 'iconic images – those that are simplified to bare meaning, such as the smiley face – allow the viewer to identify with a character to a greater extent than realistically rendered images'.[26]

Certainly, the character type of the ordinary man is central to Pixar's storytelling signature, to its authorial voice. Of the longstanding, much discussed tradition of film authorship, it's still useful to turn to the far-off time of the early 1960s when film critic Andrew Sarris defined film authorship as being concerned with 'the distinguishable personality of the director as a criterion of value. Over a group of films, a director must exhibit certain recurring characteristics of style, which serve as his signature.'[27]

Of Pixar's visual style, film scholar David Bordwell has noted that:

Like live-action editors, Pixar editors have to keep an eye on continuity of the objects in the frame. Because each shot is reworked across many phases, items of the set, lighting, colour, atmosphere, effects and rendering have to be maintained, on many layers or levels of the program. (I gather it's like the layers in PhotoShop.) Sometimes a layer, whether a prop, character, or set element, fails to 'turn on' and so a discontinuity can crop up. A finished Pixar film typically has 1,500 shots or more, so there's a lot to keep track of. In another carryover from live-action features, Pixar plots are conceived and executed in three discrete acts. It's not only a storytelling strategy but a convenience in production. Rather than waiting until the entire film is done to examine the results of the different phases, the filmmakers can finish one act ahead of the others in order to troubleshoot the rest. I've studied how filmmakers compose the image in order to shift our attention, so I was happy to hear that this process is of concern to the Pixar team. […]In looking at storyboards and animated sequences, [Bill Kinder's] colleagues sometimes use laser pointers to track the main areas of interest within shots and across cuts, especially when characters' eyelines are involved. Nice to see that sometimes academic analysis mirrors the practical decisions of filmmakers.[28]

Writing this book in 2012, it's more or less correct to describe Pixar as a pop-culture icon and a beacon for animation in particular, and dynamic, popular filmmaking more broadly. It's become trusted. Indeed, Pixar's 'It Gets Easier' video piece, which promoted tolerance towards gender difference, speaks clearly of the trust that audiences put in Pixar's sensibility.

At the beginning of 2005, Pixar was named the fifth most influential brand in America with Apple positioned at number one. Recently, however, there's been the occasional suggestion that the studio is in a creative slump, just because it's made two sequels back to back. Not so, I'd suggest. Indeed, a sequel can often improve on the original. Certainly, Walt Disney, a progenitor to the Pixar sensibility, understood the value of rebooting long-established stories, and the animation historian Michael Barrier has made the point that, 'Disney was immersed in his own dreams; what made him different and so much more exciting and interesting than most entrepreneurs was that he emerged as an artist through realising his ambitions for business.'[29]

Accessible and emotionally engaging (some would say overly manipulative, although all films manipulate, of course – that's the contract we make with a film of any type; to be stimulated to think and feel in a way that we wouldn't have done had we not sat down to watch the film), the Pixar cultural foothold and the films' meaning for audiences has been acknowledged more recently through museum exhibits and documentaries about their work. Indeed, if any further sign were needed of the degree to which Pixar's movies and characters have become a part of popular culture, their inclusion as US postage stamp images in 2011 was a pretty good index of this.

Pixar's films have emphasised the fascination and primal allure of animation, taking us into a range of 'picture-book' versions of life's dramas, doubts and wish fulfilments. Certainly, the studio's films transform reality in a distinct and particularly American way that still holds sway with large numbers of people, even if we are now living after the American century of political and cultural might and influence. It seems to suggest, too, that the storytelling mode of popular American movies remains favourable and appealing to many. Jack Zipes in *The Oxford Companion to Fairy Tales* perhaps alludes to something deep-rooted in the appeal when he notes of wonder tales that, 'They are wish fulfilments. They are obviously connected to initiation rites that introduce listeners to the "proper" way to become a member of a particular community.'[30]

OLD SCHOOL

Norman Klein, in his book *7 Minutes*, makes the compelling point that 'the earliest Mickey shorts – and early sound animation in general – differ greatly from the canon of later Disney. These cartoons, from 1928 to 1934, are anti-realist, drawn specifically for the flat screen. In short, they continued a tradition of graphic narrative which dates back to the eighteenth century, but particularly stems from nineteenth-century illustration.'[31]

Of his own sense of the world around him, Hans Christian Andersen commented that, 'Life itself is the most wonderful fairy tale.'[32] Corny though that might seem at first glance, it actually hints at the range of emotional complexities that fairy tales impart; they're more than only the happy ending.

I think its right to draw attention to, and explore further, the ways in which the films of the Pixar Animation studio accomplish some of the same storytelling effects realised by writers such as Hans Christian Andersen, Lewis Carroll (*Alice's Adventures in Wonderland*), E Nesbitt (*The Phoenix and the Carpet*), J M Barrie (*Peter Pan*), L Frank Baum (*The Wonderful Wizard of Oz*) and John Masefield (*The Box of Delights*), to name just those who are particularly well known to us. Pixar movies are Edwardian in their affinity for the experiences of boys. As Jackie Wullschlager notes in her book *Inventing Wonderland*, the Victorian era was besotted with little girls and the Edwardian era with little boys. In turn, the realm of the comic allowed a new opportunity to render larger-than-life stories. In considering animated movies, we can usefully look to the world of comics – also a form that, since the mid-1980s, has become increasingly well regarded. The novelist and essayist Michael Chabon (he wrote the screenplays for two excellent genre movies: *Spiderman 2* and *John Carter*) has explained in an essay entitled 'Kids' Stuff' that, 'Almost from the first, fitfully in the early days, intermittently through the fifties and then starting in the mid-sixties with increasing vigour and determination, a battle has been waged by writers, artists, editors and publishers to elevate the medium, to expand the scope of its subject matter and the range of its artistic styles.'[33]

Pixar is also powerfully anchored in the classical tradition of the Walt Disney studio and its productions of the 1940s, 1950s and 1960s. And we can additionally draw a line between Pixar and its Japanese contemporary, Studio Ghibli. In the 1950s, the cinema of Japan found an appreciative, if relatively small, audience in Europe and North America with the movies of Akira Kurosawa (particularly the visually exotic jidai-geki films) that helped bridge the cultural divide. Kurosawa's stories were often tales of adventure and had a sense of visual spectacle and pageantry about them. In a sense, a repeat of the emerging fascination with Japanese cinema of the 1950s has re-occurred in the early-twenty-first century through the interest in the work of Studio Ghibli and other east Asian companies, whose output has become increasingly available across Europe and America. Consider the Chinese animated feature classic *Uproar in Heaven* and how, within the relatively small orbit of the animation realm, its re-release in autumn 2012 was heralded. We might say that Miyazaki and Ghibli have become a 'shorthand' for the anime form, emblematic of it. In 2009, John Lasseter and the Japanese animator and director Hayao Miyazaki gave a press conference at which they discussed their respective new releases and also reflected on animation more broadly. Lasseter spoke of how much of an influence Miyazaki's hand-drawn animation had been in presenting the illusion of spatial depth and he cited Miyazaki's movie *Lupin* as a particularly vivid example of the staging of action.[34]

Miyazaki has become an oft-cited frame of reference for Pixar. Of his film *Spirited Away* Miyazaki observed that, 'With *Spirited Away* I wanted to say to them, "Don't worry, it will be all right in the end, there will be something for you", not just in cinema, but also in everyday life. For that it was necessary to have a heroine who was an ordinary girl, not someone who could fly or do something impossible. Just a girl you can encounter anywhere in Japan. Every time I wrote or drew something concerning the character of Chihiro and her actions, I asked myself the question whether my friend's daughter or her friends would be capable of doing it. That was my criteria for every scene in which I gave Chihiro another task or challenge. Because it's through surmounting these challenges that this little Japanese girl becomes a capable person. It took me three years to make this film, so now my friend's daughter is 13 years old rather than ten, but she still loved the film and that made me very happy.'[35] There's a sense here of recognising how animated films can resonate, and it's an attitude that Pixar would seem to be very consistent in applying both to their own work and to the way in which they generate audience interest in it at the critical moment of promotion before a theatrical release.

Certainly it seems to make sense that what Jack Zipes identifies as central to the charm and power of the ancient world of the fairy tale also resonates in the context of those films produced by Pixar Animation Studio. This tangible, identifiable 'quality', which we might just say is 'what Pixar does', is worth getting to grips with a little more and we can embark on this by marking the equation between animation and the ancient art of puppetry.

American fairy tale and folklore is delineated and parsed as follows by Linda S Watts in *Encyclopedia of American Folklore*, where she writes that folklore refers to 'transmitted traditional beliefs, myths, tales, language practices and customs of the people of the United States'.[36] A little later, she notes how 'the real power of folklore becomes clearest when happening in a culture demanding deep contemplation and considered response'.[37]

The scholar Scott Cutler Shershow has written extensively about the culture and tradition of puppets (and so, by extension, explores some of the appeal of animation), and, in his book *Puppets and Popular Culture*, he makes a point that's readily applicable to the charms and fascinations of Pixar's movies: 'In a wide variety of discourse from an extended historical period, the puppet was envisioned and re-visioned – as metaphor, meta-dramatic device, or marker of cultural subordination.'[38] Shershow also talks about puppetry being a form which allows 'the anxieties and constructions that shape our social lives'.[39]

In thinking about Pixar, and computer-animated movies more generally, it's right to recognise the place of the contemporary young audience and their familiarity with computer-game aesthetics. In my own modest experience, I've taught students on film studies courses who have, in fact, been much more knowledgeable about computer-game titles, aesthetics and history than their equivalent in terms of cinema.

At this point in time, Pixar is a studio whose name has become a highly recognisable brand and, as any brand would hope, that name has become a reason for trust on the part of the audience. There is a sense of not just a certain kind, and level, of technical quality (slickness) and accomplishment but also a sense that the ideology of the film will satisfy the audience's 'need' to witness a story. As such, Pixar is a powerful example of studio as author which, in turn, prompts the question: are the directors who work at Pixar, given the intensely collaborative nature of the medium, also authors?

Brad Bird, during promotional activity for the theatrical release of his first Pixar film, *The Incredibles*, made an observation that suggests some useful connections: 'Walt Disney has cast such a long shadow over animation, and Disney itself was more of a producer's studio than a director's studio. That has helped [encourage] the idea that [animation] is a process, rather than an art that's guided by a vision. Walt Disney was in effect the director of those great films. He wasn't a good director when he was [literally] directing, as a viewing of any of the few short films he's credited as director make clear, but he was an excellent director in terms of directing his directors. But I think that notion, that it's a system that creates an animated film, and not a person, has been kind of bound up in how people perceive animation. The John Lasseters and the Miyazakis of the world are in the minority. For the most part, we have films that are directed by two or three guys, and which one is the author?'[40]

Since the release of Pixar's first feature film (*Toy Story*), there have been a number of useful, in-depth looks at the studio's technological processes, and, whilst these are key to the creativity and industry of the place, with this book I hope to suggest some connection between Pixar's storytelling conventions and those of wonder tales, folk tales and fairy tales. Pixar's films function as contemporary folk stories using a medium that has particular popular currency. To some degree, then, my interest has less to do with what the filmmaker's proposed intention has been (is this the downside of the DVD Director's Commentary tradition?) and more to do with what qualities seem to evidently connect with a longer, wider storytelling tradition. Why do stories work? That's the big question and one that we, understandably, sort of take for granted because of the very familiar place that storytelling occupies in each of our lives. Certainly, the Pixar films have a connection to the stories collected by the Brothers Grimm. These stories continue to matter. Of the Grimms' stories, Alison Lurie has written that, 'The heroes and heroines of Grimms' tales and other traditional collections usually meet their reward on earth.'[41]

PIXAR AND THE AMERICAN ANIMATION RENAISSANCE

In 1986 the glimmers of a soon-to-follow upswing in the creative and commercial fortunes of the American feature-length animated film manifested themselves. In December of 1986 Universal Pictures released the Don Bluth-directed, Steven Spielberg-produced *An American Tail*. It was the most commercially successful American animated film that had been released theatrically up to that moment. In the summer of 1988, Spielberg and Robert Zemeckis collaborated on the classic *Who Framed Roger Rabbit?* And, in the autumn, Disney released the popular *Oliver and Co* and Spielberg and Lucas had *The Land Before Time*. In 1989 Disney released *The Little Mermaid*, followed in 1991 by *Beauty and the Beast*, *Aladdin* in 1992 and *The Lion King* in 1994. In the book *Prime Time Animation: Television Animation and American Culture* we read, in the introduction, a discussion of the cult American animated TV series, *Beavis and Butt Head* (1992–97), which is considered to have played a critical part at the time in establishing a renewed interest for audiences in animation, both on TV and at the cinema. Hence, we read that '*Beavis and Butt Head*, along with the renaissance in television animation, inaugurated by *The Simpsons* in 1990, offers a rich site for understanding prime time television and the effects of cable television on the wider field of cultural production'.[42]

The book then makes the further point – relevant in some ways to the experience of Pixar and the broader spectrum of the American animated feature film – that 'Disney brought the constraints and devices of drama and narrative to bear on the field of animation, containing the exuberance of earlier examples of the form by privileging story and character over the inherent plasticity of the form'.[43]

It was out of this enriching animation culture and industry of the early 1990s that Pixar found a foothold. Whilst these films were being released, the studio was producing short films and commercials and moving towards a point of critical mass where it was able to begin considering its first feature flm. Whereas the movies mentioned a moment ago were all cel animated (pencil drawings rendered as painted characters on acetate and laid over painted backgrounds) or, in the case of *Who Framed Roger Rabbit?*, integrated dynamically with live-action material, Pixar was viewing the capacities of the computer-animated film.

The Disney connection has been a part of Pixar's economic and organisational identity and has also informed some of the sense we have about the creative qualities of its material. In early 2006, Disney bought Pixar, causing animation fans, who felt protective towards the company, which they viewed as an independent production entity now in the apparent control of a large entertainment corporation, to voice their reservations. There's a healthy fan exchange of ideas about films in development and production at Pixar, allowing the prospective audience to flex their own creative ideas and versions of what the eventual film might be. Indeed, to place Pixar in the longer historical timeline, we could say that their films are more attuned with the sensibility of Disney's *Silly Symphonies* short films than, say, the heritage of Mickey Mouse.[44] Whatever the answer, there's little doubt that animation is perhaps now, more than ever, enjoying established popularity and ever-increasing credibility.

In September 2012, Dreamworks Animation announced a very intense production schedule for 2012–16, listing ten feature films that were moving through production for release during this timeframe: an immense volume of production activity. This spoke, in part, of the continued commercial power of the computer-animated movie around the world.[45]

At CinemaCon (a trade gathering for North American cinema owners) in April 2012, excitement was stirred by announcements of upcoming Pixar projects to be released in the year or two after this book is published: Pete Docter's 'mind' film, Lee Unkrich's Muerte festival film (*Unkrich*) and Bob Peterson's *The Good Dinosaur*. Online film-fan excitement regarding these announced projects was as predictable as Big Ben striking on time. It's fair to say that Pixar offers an active example of how fan communities and animation enthusiasts relate to each other and perceive themselves, both in their own right and in relation to the films which they claim a very personal stake in. And Pixar's has been an endlessly considered film production outfit; just look at how *Time Out* magazine took the chance to weigh up Pixar and Studio Ghibli in terms of which produced the more dynamic work.[46]

In understanding the allure of the Pixar movie, there's a rewarding connection to make with the fantasy-film successes of a number of films produced in the 1970s and 1980s. These are films that many of the Pixar staff would be very familiar with, informing their sense of characterisation, plot, tone and subject choice. Indeed, of the filmmakers synonymous with the fantasy film, we must cite George Lucas and Steven Spielberg – and, critically, both expressed strong feelings towards the tradition of the Disney studio's animated films of the 1940s and 1950s.

Back in September 2010, Pixar released online images from an abandoned movie it had been developing entitled *Newt*. The online expressions of regret generated by the news that the film would not be made, based on these conceptual images, was telling of a sincere audience fascination with not just the end product but also with the studio's creative process.

In 2008, Ed Catmull wrote an essay in the *Harvard Business Review* about his experience of managing a company whose business was creative product. His comments attest to the precision of the animation form as an expression of thought: 'A movie contains literally tens of thousands of ideas. They're in the form of every sentence; in the performance of each line; in the design of characters, sets, and backgrounds; in the locations of the camera; in the colours, the lighting, the pacing. The director and the other creative leaders of a production do not come up with all the ideas on their own; rather, every single member of the 200- to 250-person production group makes suggestions. Creativity must be present at every level of every artistic and technical part of the organisation. The leaders sort through a mass of ideas to find the ones that fit into a coherent whole – that support the story – which is a very difficult task. It's like an archaeological dig where you don't know what you're looking for or whether you will even find anything. The process is downright scary.'[47]

Catmull's sketch of the realities of his work is so very useful as it openly acknowledges that a film is not something that is somehow easily thrown together without thought. Choices are made and perhaps nowhere more so than in the animated film. That doesn't mean that what the producer intended is the only response an audience can have, however, and that's key to our relationship with movies. Put it this way: I don't need to know what Shakespeare intended in terms of 'meaning' when he wrote his stage plays.

In terms of the mainstream animated feature film, even now, animation is still held (by some producers and many review pages) to be largely synonymous with the idea of kids' stuff, as though it's less substantial or worth getting 'right' than content for adults. This is a damning indictment of how our culture perceives the material it produces for young people: as though it's somehow less worthy than material for adults. Surely, though, there could be no more important an audience?

The general ignorance of the diversity of forms found in animation as an expressive form means that a vast ocean of invention and creativity, not aimed at children, is overlooked, particularly, perhaps, in the popular American tradition.

The spirit of invention that often characterises animation potentially imbues it with an inherent creative joy no matter how crude the rendering might be. Animation wilfully subverts the accepted physical laws of the world; and, in doing so, it can turn on its head much of how we see the world. Animation makes the familiar unfamiliar, allowing for a fresh view of what we know, of what we take for granted.

The opportunity, then, for animation to tell fantastic stories is very particular. It is the one form of cinema that can be more designed and planned than any other. The huge cost and labour implications of many forms of animation mean that getting all of the story elements effectively measured and calibrated for the most emotional and intellectual effect is paramount. Even editing animated films is a different process to editing live action. In live action, the director would typically cover action from a number of angles and would choose what works best during the edit phase. Not so the animated film where these decisions are mapped out and agreed in pre-production.

Animation, then, has yielded a startling diversity of forms, from the most highly resourced and widely distributed to the most bareboned productions with the narrowest of audiences.

Like all the best fantasy stories and scenarios, animation needs reality. But then, maybe, reality needs animation. Indeed, this notion of the redemptive possibilites of the imagination and the spirit of the fanciful has been central to cultural life of every kind, in every place and every age, and it makes the connection back to the deeper well of storytelling. In his magnificent book, *The Origin of Stories*, Brian Boyd writes that 'nature has shaped our ultra-social selves to attend to character and event in life and story'.[48]

In Japan, Kido Shiro, head of Kamata Shochiku Studios back in 1924, said that, 'To inspire despair in our viewers would be unforgivable. The bottom line is that the basis of film must be salvation.'[49]

For psychologist Bruno Bettelheim, in his landmark book *The Uses of Enchantment: The Meaning and Importance of Fairy Tales* (1977), there is an exciting relationship to be understood between the minds of young children and the natural, animal world around them. For Bettelheim, this relationship is dampened and suppressed by adult life. In effect, it is this animistic aspect of our minds that informs and gives so much animation its appeal. For Bettelheim,

'Subjected to the rational teachings of others, the child only buries his "true knowledge" deeper in his soul and it remains untouched by rationality, but it can be formed and informed by what fairy tales have to say.'[50]

The wonder tales that characterise ancient cultures worldwide tend to centre on a narrative of a simple boy taken advantage of by others. However, the simple boy's goodness sees him right in the end.

Animation, then, is both super-ancient and ultra modern in its combination of forms and attitudes.

There are differences to note between myths, fairy tales and folk tales. We might say that Pixar works especially well as folk tale, and its popularity early on prompted Ellen Wolff to write a piece entitled 'Firms Plan CGI Pix for Infinity and Beyond'.[51]

Typically, animation seems to contain rich possibilities in expressing what we might broadly term fairy tale stories (or wonder tales), or stories that possess those kinds of qualities. Critically, the form is very much about visualising transformation amd various kinds of 'magic' (of which filmmaking is itself one), about making something move and live that could not do so by itself. So many animated films explore this motif of transformation. Marina Warner has written of the fairy tale that 'magic will vanish with too much rationalisation, and fairy tales derive their power from the enigma of enchantment'.[52]

In the larger scale of things, the animated film has, for the longest time, been associated with an idea of childhood. It's what we might think of as nostalgia, and certainly there is a nostalgia culture and industry which many films tap into in their conceptual development and their marketing. They are informed by, and then inform, a circle of exchange, the nostalgia sensibility. In the book *American Comedy* there's a cautious description of what nostalgia is and does: 'Nostalgia works by simplifying the past, removing all contradiction and nuances in favour of an oft-told narrative of innocence lost.'[53]

Indeed, the way in which cinema has presented the experience of being a child has a rich and fascinating tradition and, in her book *Childhood and Cinema*, Vicky leBeau writes that 'cinema [is] closer to perception, it can come closer to the child...'[54]

The connection of film and dream has been long talked about and enjoyed, and animation's elasticity allows it to be anti-realistic with ease. Of the dream and film connection we read: 'The idea of a connection between film and dreams seems to be grounded in Freud's theories. The father of psychoanalysis stated that dreams dramatise ideas. The so-called dream-work must produce a visual representation of the dream-thoughts – and dramatisation for Freud is the transformation of a thought into a visual situation.'[55]

Animation's other affinity with the literary fairy tale and folk-story tradition is in the way that it places importance on the expressive potential of anthropomorphism, whereby animals and non-human objects and entities are lent more human characteristics, both in terms of face and body, and in their modes of expression. *Aesop's Fables* accomplished this task brilliantly and storytelling's never looked back.

Animation has a facility for expressing mystery and for conjuring the numinous, a quality that gets so easily trampled by our so-called 'enlightened' era. Animation functions as the latest iteration of a visual-storytelling, illustrative spirit that creativity has always nurtured ever since humans drew bison and ibex in the firelight of caves. Importantly, though, animation is not solely the province of fantasy and adventure stories that have been derived from a comic-strip way of imagining the world. The animation of the 1930s and 1940s, which largely established an expectation of what the form could be, has been criticised for sustaining stereotypes about gender and the idea of otherness as represented through physical and behavioural tics.

The sense of free association that animation has so finely developed is what makes the material work. More recently, and famously, we can refer to *Waltz With Bashir* (Ari Folman, 2008) and *Persepolis* (Marjane Satrapi, 2007) as animated movies that were incredibly real in their subject matter, but treated it in vivid, inventive ways.

Myths, legends, fairy tales and other more ancient artworks are all imbued with images of monsters, halflings, gods, goddesses and fabulous landscapes that map the human soul. It's one of the joys of cinema that the fairy tales and stories of legend have been so readily appropriated by animation. For all that live action can achieve, animation is the most elastic and free form of the cinematic traditions. To borrow from Paul Klee, animation allows the filmmaker to take a line for a very emotive and intriguing walk.

By the middle of the twentieth century, cinema was considered to be a key way of socialising children, and animation played a significant part in this process. In the West, film has heavily influenced people's sense of, and reception of, fairy tales. Certainly, the films of Walt Disney have led the way in this and many others have developed the engagement further. However, it is critical here to note that the animated fairy tale, as adaptation or by association of style, is not limited to the mainstream American film. It's an issue of credibility, though: many still associate animated films with the most disposable examples of cinema.

Animation, then, can operate allegorically, politically, and psychologically and often without us immediately recognising it. This is the something that Brad Bird alludes to in the quotation that you'll find at the very beginning of this chapter.

The word animation is tightly bound up with notions of the miraculous, of breathing life into something lifeless. Richard Thompson notes in his vivid essay, *Meep Meep*, that 'American animation, like American comic strips, was full of weird, twisted, surreal versions of the world, impossible to capture with real life photography. It was powered by glorious primitivism, unlike the increasingly sophisticated live action film.'[56]

Once upon a time, the American writer L Frank Baum, author of *The Wonderful Wizard of Oz*, made an astute and enduring observation, saynig that 'I believe that dreams – day dreams... with your eyes wide open... are likely to lead to the betterment of the world. The imaginative child will become the imaginative man or woman most apt to create, to invent and therefore foster civilisation. A prominent educator tells me that fairy tales are of untold value in developing imagination in the young.'[57]

In the most vividly wrought of Pixar films, the sensibility that Baum refers to is manifested in the characterisations (of animals, objects, people), and, for the writer Ed Hooks, 'Personality and action are not mutually exclusive.'[58] Certainly, the expressive power of Pixar's movies have brought them massive popular success and, as such, it seems to be worth our time to pay closer attention to how this power is engineered. As 'blockbusters', Pixar's films function as very promising examples of what this 'kind' of movie can achieve. Pertinently, film journalist Manohla Dargis wrote of blockbuster cinema that 'if audiences dig spectacle, critics often view it with suspicion, as sneers about the modern blockbuster suggest. The negative rap on blockbusters is partly due to the literary bent of a lot of critics, who privilege words over images and tend to review screenplays, or what's left of them, rather than the amalgamation of sights and sounds in front of them.'[59]

Contrastingly, the fairy tale scholar Jack Zipes has expressed deep reservations about the mainstream sensibility, and longer-standing tradition, that Pixar's movies function within, saying that, 'For the most part, when Americans think of fairy tales (and, to a certain extent, this is also a global phenomenon), they think of Disney. Thanks to the theme parks and the commodities that are produced [and the strength of the Disney brand], you can't help but think of fairy tales in light of the way the Disney Corporation has interpreted them. And in my mind, once you've seen one Disney film, you've seen them all: they repeat the plots; their self-produced animated films tend to be very conventional; and I think there's no experimentation whatsoever, no breaking away from the plot formulations... It's just boring, at least for me, to see these films... And most animators who have worked with Disney have always wanted to be the one to illustrate the evil characters, because at least they're more interesting and more complicated. That doesn't mean that one should write off all the Disney films – I don't mean to dismiss these films [entirely] – but they represent the worst aspects of capitalist, corporate productions.'[60]

STRUCTURE OF THE BOOK

This book sets out to offer the reader a one-stop guide to Pixar's work, exploring each film in terms of creative choices made as evidenced by the work on screen. The book also hopes to make some connections to the larger span of animation history, animation culture and genre filmmaking. This book, then, proposes that Pixar is as much an auteur as an individual film director might be considered to be. There's a point to be made, too, about how the directors of Pixar's films bring to the material their own idiosyncracies. The studio's invention, and its commitment to the fantastical as a way of exploring such familiar feelings and matters of the heart, have been vital to its popularity and, in the pages that follow, I hope to give some sense of how these effects are achieved and why they resonate. Film, and computer gaming, are dominant expressive modes in the early twenty-first century, animation forming a fascinating bridge between them, and in both formats there's an opportunity to tell stories that are both inward and outwardly expansive.

Each film is allocated a chapter that breaks down into a consideration of its conceptual origin and development, design and storytelling influences, connections to other movies and cultural reference points, dramatic interest and , finally, how the film fared with audiences. Underpinning the discussion of all of the films is the idea that the Pixar films are a part of an enduring American fairy tale tradition.

THE FILMS

Toy Story (1995)

Directed by: John Lasseter
Written by: John Lasseter, Andrew Stanton, Pete Docter, Joe Ranft (story and screenplay), Joss Whedon, Joel Cohen and Alec Sokolow (screenplay)
Produced by: Bonnie Arnold, Ralph Guggenheim
Music by: Randy Newman
Edited by: Robert Gordon, Lee Unkrich
Art Direction: Ralph Eggleston
Cast: Tom Hanks (Woody), Tim Allen (Buzz Lightyear), Don Rickles (Mr Potato head), Jim Varney (Slinky Dog), Wallace Shawn (Rex), John Ratzenberger (Hamm), Annie Potts (Bo Peep), Wayne Knight (Al), John Morris (Andy Davis), Laurie Metcalf (Andy's Mom), Estelle Harris (Mrs Potato Head)

Human culture is rich with stories charting our long-running fascination with automata and other artificial figures (notably, sculpture) that seek to replicate the appearance and movements of people and animals. Martin Scorsese's beautifully realised, and rather delicate, adaptation of Brian Selznick's book *The Invention of Hugo Cabret* was a very recent explicit example and we can also look to *Pinocchio* and also the Olympia sequence in the fantasy movie *The Tales of Hoffmann* (Michael Powell and Emeric Pressburger, 1952). Intriguingly, Powell had long wanted to make an animated film at some point in his career. Alas, that fantasy never became real. So the idea that a kind of enchantment might allow an otherwise motionless and lifeless object to 'come alive' underpins the animation aesthetic in a vivid way. The prospect of toys coming to life is not a new instance of wish-fulfilment. We can trace the tradition back to a number of stories in print and moving pictures, titles such as *The Steadfast Tin Soldier* by Hans Christian Andersen. Of Andersen, Alison Lurie has written, in a way that rhymes with the Pixar vibe, that 'like a child, Andersen saw everything in the world as alive and conscious. In his stories not only animals and birds, but also bugs and toys and flowers and even household objects have complete human personalities.'[61]

In a rather matter-of-fact way, the following note appeared in a 1993 edition of *Cinefex*, a visual effects magazine, which was profiling a relatively little-known studio of the time, named Pixar. The piece focused on the studio's commercials work but also noted that Pixar was working on its first feature-length project, described only as 'a seventy-five-minute, action adventure story to be done completely with 3D graphics'.[62] Ultimately, this unspecified project would become known to audiences, just over two years later, as *Toy Story*, a film that would vividly confirm that computer animation had reached a watershed moment, with cinema beginning to shift away from being only about photographing the real world. At the time, cinema was announcing a new iteration of itself: virtual cinema with more in common perhaps with painting than with photography.

It's fascinating to go back and read material published just before the original theatrical release of *Toy Story*. In the 1993 *Cinefex* magazine article mentioned a moment ago, the writer Estelle Shay begins her profile of Pixar by placing it in the following context: 'With the unveiling of Steven Spielberg's current blockbuster, *Jurassic Park* (1993), computer-generated imaging has taken a quantum leap that may forever change the way effects movies are made. Although an appreciation of CGI and its vast potential has been steadily growing, most people, including many in the effects industry, were wholly unprepared for the astonishing realism of *Jurassic Park*'s digital dinosaurs. Most, but not all.'[63] This excerpt marks the moment when producers and audiences were recognising a new technology and, in *Jurassic Park*, the scene in which the scientists first sight a living, breathing, stomping dinosaur is visually stunning and emotionally spectacular; characters and audiences perfectly matched as both the story world and the world of the cinema witness new technology. Spielberg achieved this elusive fusion, and so have Pixar.

And so to the origins of Pixar's watershed moment in feature film production. *Toy Story* can be said to have had a partial beginning in a decision made at Pixar (following the awards success and industry recognition accorded the *Luxo Jr* and *Tin Toy* shorts) that the company should progress from its established work in short films and commercials to producing a 30-minute TV special. Surprisingly, Disney's then-vice president of animation, Peter Schneider, suggested that Pixar move straight into producing a feature project. As such, Pixar signed a three-picture deal with Disney, setting in motion what has become a major partnership, not only in terms of the dynamics of film economics and the industrial processes aspect, but also in terms of how the storytelling example of one studio (Disney) has influenced that of another. Of the Disney name, brand and style, it has been described by Eric Smoodin thus: 'With the release of *Fantasia*... Disney came to be perceived as the consummate artist, the perfect combination of the corporate and the creative.'[64]

Certainly, Pixar's own short film, *Tin Toy*, contained the germ of what became the more expansive *Toy Story* concept, namely the emotional secret life of a toy. Broadly speaking, it's a scenario that we might recognise from the work of other, older fabulists. John Lasseter has explained that 'I always thought there was a lot of potential in a story about toys that are alive. We started to explore that idea in *Tin Toy* – but it really came together in *Toy Story*.'[65] Lasseter's comment rather understates the challenge involved in making the leap from short to feature.

Speaking about the challenges of computer imaging, visual effects supervisor Richard Edlund (who was pivotal to the age of both optical and digital effects, his credits embracing the optical-age wonders of *Poltergeist* [Tobe Hooper, 1982] and *The Empire Strikes Back* [Irvin Kershner, 1980] and the digital-age awe of the films *Spiderman* [Sam Raimi, 2002] and *Spiderman 2* [Sam Raimi, 2004]) once made a critical observation that's relevant to us here. He said that 'the thing about computer animation is that you have to intellectualise the serendipitous blip'.[66] Although Edlund is making a general statement about the visual-effects production process and its various aesthetic challenges, it's an understanding that's fully applicable to the world of Pixar's movies and computer-animated or computer-generated films more broadly.

For all its digital allure, *Toy Story*'s narrative is steeped in old-world traditions of narrative structure, character and animation technique. As with many films that impact vividly on us, *Toy Story* centres around a simple plot which allows real breathing space for the development of atmosphere and of character. In a sense, we might say that the images have space to linger.

The events of *Toy Story*, then, follow a proven and powerful narrative line. As such, it's a film that well understands genre traditions.

In 1993, two years before the release of *Toy Story*, Ralph Guggenheim, vice president of the nascent animation division at Pixar, explained that 'ten or fifteen years ago you would not have considered making a feature-length film of this nature because the "ink and paint" portion, or the rendering part of the process, would have taken too long.'[67] Guggenheim's reality check now seems like a relic from ancient history, but it illustrates well the evolutionary leap that *Toy Story* represented, and its subsequent commercial success then validated the possibility of CGI as a format worth investing in.

Almost two decades since its original release, *Toy Story* continues to stand as a landmark movie and as a touchstone for producers of computer-animated feature films. It's a film that symbolises what constitutes a financially well-resourced American film industry operating at its storytelling best.

Having been crucial to the evolution of the computer-animated short film, John Lasseter applied this experience to *Toy Story*, his feature-film directing and screenwriting debut, and the project's four-year production period inevitably confronted Lasseter and his colleagues with the challenges arising from how best to craft coherent and engaging characters and narrative mechanics whilst also making the wisest and most aesthetically dynamic use of the available technology. In terms of what we sometimes expect of popular American cinema. *Toy Story* offers us both something novel and something familiar in artful combination. In 1987, Lasseter published an article entitled 'Principles of Traditional Animation Applied to 3D Animation' in the journal *Computer Animation*. Lasseter stated that many established rules of animation could be applied to the aesthetics of the brave new world of computer animation. Certainly, *Toy Story* makes real Lasseter's 'prophecy'. Of the fluidity between approaches, both traditional and contemporary, Pixar's picture editor Ken Schretzman commented about the dynamic of the studio's typical production process that 'at one point in the film, part of it's in storyboard, part of it's in layout, some of it is animated, some of it's being rendered, while some of the scenes are being rewritten.'[68]

An additional challenge in the production of *Toy Story*, and one which served to extend and deepen the creative palette of Pixar, was the creation of believably illuminated and shaded surface, applied to the illusion of everything from animal fur, to bedclothes, to the surface textures of toys. In effect, the studio was grappling with visual realism in a way that Renaissance painters had done.

Toy Story's characters all have very shiny surfaces that reflect light – a smart, common-sense decision by the production in that, at the time, plastic-looking surfaces were 'easily' achievable on the computer. The believable illusion of human skin would require the seasoning of a little more time and, hence, it was not until 2004 that *The Incredibles*, Pixar's first human-centred movie, was released.

In tandem with the refinement of various technical tools, the production of *Toy Story* moved forward with script development. In 1989, Disney had released its hugely popular adaptation of Hans Christian Andersen's *The Little Mermaid* (1989). Produced under the supervision of then-studio chief Jeffrey Katzenberg, the project's production was notable for being based around a fully realised screenplay, just as a live-action feature would be. Prior to this there had been a tendency in animation production to develop feature films from storyboarding only.

For *Toy Story*, the writing team, which comprised Joss Whedon, Pete Docter, Andrew Stanton, Joel Cohen, Alex Sokolow and Joe Ranft, developed the film's storyline and from there wrote a number of full screenplay drafts. The screenplay's development happened in tandem with the generation of conceptual artwork for the characters, and eventually the storyboard of the film. This ongoing dialogue engaged the team in how best to create a dynamic between words and pictures. Typical of the long-established production pipeline convention for animated films, once the screenplay for *Toy Story* began to narrow in focus, the process began of mapping out the entire story using hand-drawn storyboards. At this point, drawings and painted character designs were also used as the basis for maquettes of the characters which were then scanned into the computer, just as Ed Catmull and Alvy Ray Smith had done at the University of Utah in 1972.

Typical of the screenplay's development phase was the emergence and subsequent abandonment of various story elements, some of which would be rebooted for use in later Pixar films. Certainly, there's a good lesson here for aspiring writers: in writing, nothing's ever really wasted. Perhaps the best example of this healthy recycling of story, and its renewable energy, is that *Toy Story* was supposed to have opened with a Buzz Lightyear cartoon. Whilst this 'prologue' was abandoned, it was essentially revisited at the beginning of *Toy Story 2*.

One of the key aesthetic choices made in developing *Toy Story*, and it was a choice that ran counter to the established narrative (and plot) tradition of Disney animated features, was the absence of any ambition to make it an animated musical. Somewhat amusingly, during *Toy Story*'s production an executive at Disney questioned Pixar about where they would be putting the eight songs through which the characters would express their hopes and fears. Pixar explained that they would be using dialogue alone to communicate these things. In designing *Toy Story*'s narrative and visual palette, one of the key aesthetic impulses for John Lasseter was that 'we wanted to create a sense of nostalgia for the adults in the audience'.[69] For sure, this declaration of a nostalgic spirit provides an insight into not just *Toy Story*'s allure, but also the studio's subsequent output.

Certainly, Pixar's films are bound together by an essentially bright and radiant visual style. A key influence on the Pixar look for *Toy Story* was the artwork of American painter Maxfield Parrish. Parrish was noted for his hyperreal paintings, which included pieces such as *Riverbank Autumn* (1938), an image that appears to shine with some inner glow. It's a visual style that has even more of an impact on *A Bug's Life*, the film Pixar made after *Toy Story*. Parrish was also noted for his paintings of fairies and other larger-than-life scenarios.

In concocting the principal characters for *Toy Story*, each of which related to and reinforced an established pop-culture icon (the cowboy, the astronaut and the powerful American idea of the frontier), John Lasseter noted that 'because of the popularity of *Jurassic Park*, we knew we had to have a dinosaur'.[70] John Lasseter has explained how, initially, Buzz, whose original name was Lunar Larry, was conceived as more of a Dudley Do-Right kind of figure. However, through Tim Allen's vocal performance, he became imbued with something more bossy and authoritarian.

With the screenplay and storyboard context defined and approved, the production turned to recording the vocal performances of the characters.

Critical to the sonic storytelling appeal of Pixar's feature films has been their use of established film and TV stars as vocal performers for the characters – and, intriguingly, these animated characters have become as important to the perception of the film's stars as any other non-animated film roles they may have essayed.

It's an established and understandable way of producing an expensive animated film to place recognisable, familiar voice-talent in key roles. At the time of taking on the role of Woody Pride for the original *Toy Story*, Tom Hanks had established himself as a major Hollywood star, having appeared in films such as *Splash* (Ron

Howard, 1984), *Big* (Penny Marshall, 1988), *Sleepless in Seattle* (Nora Ephron, 1993), *Philadelphia* (Jonathan Demme, 1993), *Forrest Gump* (Robert Zemeckis, 1994) and *Apollo 13* (Ron Howard, 1995). To the character of Woody, Hanks brought an expected warmth and sincerity, and also a necessarily strong comic sensibility. Of comedy, Hanks has made the point that 'I guess the comic is something of a solitary figure...'[71]

In looking at development art for the character of Woody, it's intriguing to see the various possible choices that could have been made for the character. Jeff Pidgeon's early pencil drawing of Woody makes him look very vexed and more comical than in his final form, whilst Bud Luckey's illustration of the character has him sitting down, as if he's just dropped down by intention or accident, and he just looks wistful, an expression he often displays in the movies. Indeed, as a reference for the character of Woody, a doll was made up out of parts of other toys to allow the animators a better sense of scale and movement in service of the film's guiding realistic sensibility.

Alongside Hanks, the other star name showcased in *Toy Story* was the comic actor Tim Allen who voiced the character of Buzz Lightyear. By late 1995, Allen was known to many TV viewers as the star of the American sitcom *Home Improvement* (made by Disney), in which he played a regional TV star and presenter of a home improvement show, who was also shown navigating a family life he was never able to fix. Buzz Lightyear's bravado echoes that of Allen's character in *Home Improvement*, and of his role as a space ranger, and Buzz's relationship to Woody, Allen noted that 'they accept each other's limitations.'[72]

It's interesting to note that the earlier Pixar films arguably used more famous actors in lead roles than they do now. As the studio's own name as a trusted brand has become increasingly strong, star names have become less prominent in lead roles. The Pixar story style stands on its own two feet.

One advantage (and occasionally it can be a liberty that needs reining in) of computer-camera moves (virtual positioning) is that they can be completely free ranging, unencumbered by real spatial limitations. As with the Lasseter-Keane proof-of-concept experiment of 1982, adapting part of Maurice Sendak's *Where the Wild Things Are*, *Toy Story* takes creative advantage of computer graphics' virtual space and freedom for the 'camera' to move with the sort of dynamism that doesn't necessarily have to accord with the actual laws of space and motion. It's worth noting, too, that the Disney animated feature *Basil the Great Mouse Detective* (Ron Clements and Burny Mattinson, 1986) is significant for how it showcases the integration of cel animation with computer-rendered backgrounds. This is, of course, a characteristic of the Pixar films that followed. For *Toy Story*, a decision was made to make the virtual camera positions share a sensibility with live-action camera set ups, so that none of the framing appeared too 'cartoony'. In using the term 'cartoony' we might refer to the kinds of angles and perspectives created for views across the kitchen in a *Tom and Jerry* cartoon or , indeed, in the fabulous opening sequence of *Who Framed Roger Rabbit?* (Robert Zemeckis, 1988).

For *Toy Story* , a virtual crane camera was built inside the camera which allowed the crew to select the kind of virtual lenses they wanted to use for each shot, achieving a sense of movement through space that's very dynamic and which has always been a notable characteristic of the Pixar chase-sequence style: just think of Remy's running around the kitchen in *Ratatouille*.

Extensively storyboarded, one of the key reference materials used in building the tension and dynamic of the sequence that forms the prelude of the film was the train chase seen at the end of the glorious *Back to the Future Part III* (Robert Zemeckis, 1990). Other films referenced for the *Toy Story* sequence were *Ben Hur* (William Wyler, 1957), *Bullitt* (Peter Yates, 1968) and *Raiders of the Lost Ark* (Steven Spielberg, 1981), each an instance of characterisation being maintained amidst spectacular kinetic action and thunderous noise.

Toy Story begins with the now famous *Toy Story* clouds against a blue sky. We might guess we're outside, but the camera pulls back to reveal Andy playing with his toys. Andy holds Mr Potato

Head and has him holding up a cardboard-box bank. It's a Western scenario (and the opening sequence of *Toy Story 3* elaborates on this idea hugely). By playing with them, Andy is animating his toys and, in an extreme close-up, we see Woody's face as the camera pulls back and we see Andy's arm operating him. On the soundtrack we hear the song 'You Got A Friend In Me' being performed. Whilst Pixar chose not to have characters singing within the worlds they inhabit, the role of song in extending the story and enriching character remains a part of the Pixar approach. We watch as Andy then takes Woody downstairs and, in this moment, we're offered the first indication that Woody is 'alive'. The camera circles him lying down, looking blank. There is then a cut and we get Woody's point of view as he looks at Andy and his mother. This briefly held shot suggests that this toy is alive. Woody Pride (if ever such a name spoke of a character flaw, this would be it). Andy then goes back upstairs, leaving Woody there and returning shortly with his baby sister Molly. There is then a cut and the camera now closes in on Woody, who has run frantically back upstairs, lying on Andy's bed, as he wakes up, sunlight all around. Woody calls out that the 'coast is clear' and all of the toys in the room wake up. The film's smart, self-aware humour is immediately evident in the nifty sight gag in which Mr Potato Head resembles a Picasso painting. This scene establishes that the toys take it as their job to be toys, just as the monsters in *Monsters, Inc* have a job to do of being monstrous. These are 'everyman' fantasy characters. In this scene establishing the supporting toy characters, we even see Woody blush when he talks with Bo Peep (whose reflective surface recalls that attention to detail in *Tin Toy*). Woody then explains to everyone that they have just one week left before Andy moves house and so each toy must have a moving buddy. Suburbia is a setting that has come to symbolise a certain sense of innocence and order, and it's a starting point for a larger-than-life, disruptive experience to follow. One has only to watch TV series such as *The Wonder Years* and *Happy Days*, or feature films such as *ET*, *Poltergeist*, *Super 8*, *The Goonies*, *Monster House*, *Back to the Future*, *Gremlins*, *Explorers* and *Pretty In Pink*, to see this at work.

Woody makes the trilogy-spanning point that 'what matters is that we're here for Andy when he needs us'. Woody's gestures, such as the tilt of his head, play out in medium close-up, and the performance rendered by the animators is really affecting. The community of toys is duly gathered together by Woody, and the toy soldiers are sent downstairs to see what toys Andy has received as presents for his birthday, in the fear that the new toys might replace the older crop. The action involving the soldiers hiding out in a houseplant is wittily rendered as a war movie genre scene. The soldiers' movements are believable in that they don't separate from their bases but can only pivot on them in order to move. Sure enough, Andy is given a new toy, an astronaut space ranger named Buzz Lightyear. The kids arrive for the party and there is a brief, quickly edited sequence in which the toys try to see if any of the presents pose a threat to their popularity. All seems fine until Andy is given his Buzz Lightyear toy, which we don't see in detail for a minute or two. We only see the silhouette of the packaging.

Andy and his friends then charge upstairs to his room to play, and the toys scatter and hide (recalling the toys hiding from the marauding baby in *Tin Toy*). In due course, the kids are called downstairs for food, and, when the coast is clear, the toys emerge. Woody climbs up onto the bed. The camera pulls back from a close-up on his face as he looks up, aghast. The camera continues tracking back between Buzz's legs and then booms up to Buzz's face. It's an elegant, dynamic, storytelling camera move that refines the fluidity of the work that John Lasseter and Glen Keane achieved way back in 1983 when they produced the cel animation/computer-generated image, proof-of-concept sequence that adapted part of the book *Where the Wild Things Are*. We hear Woody gulp as he is confronted by the apparent usurper. When Andy later leaves Buzz on his bed, Woody confronts the new toy, suspicious of Buzz's appeal. Woody subsequently expends much energy trying to convince the toys that Buzz is not quite what he thinks. Amusingly, Buzz believes that he really is an intergalactic superhero, trying to contact Star Command. Woody tries to convince him otherwise and the film's humorous, and ultimately moving, riff on self-perception kicks off.

Buzz actually thinks the landscape of the bed is the landscape of a new planet. Woody then makes Buzz demonstrate flight, and a series of humorous physical gags ensues which prompts Buzz to think he can indeed fly. As Woody explains to the other toys that Buzz is a toy, Buzz looks crestfallen in the background as Woody's exasperated explanation plays out in the foreground. Woody's brow furrows comically as he insists that he's 'still Andy's favourite toy'. The evidence appears to prove the opposite as Andy plays with Buzz much more, and Randy Newman's song, 'Strange Things Are Happening', elaborates on Woody's sense of falling from favour. We see Woody at night, his forlorn face in the blue moonlight as he goes to sleep inside the toy chest.

The next day, the toys watch Sid, the next-door neighbour. Whereas Andy is wholesome and generous to his toys, Sid is not, and we see that he has strapped a firework to the back of a Combat Carl toy. Sid's vicious-looking dog, Scud, is also introduced in this scene. Andy and his mother then get ready to go out for pizza and, in a rather brilliant example of Pixar's story structuring, a scene follows in which Woody, envious of Buzz's popularity, accidentally sends Buzz out of the bedroom window. The toys chastise Woody for his unkind behaviour and so Woody begins to pay the price for letting his jealousy get the better of him.

Rather like *Cars*, this is a story about growing up and the lesson of humility. Andy comes to get Buzz to take him to Pizza Planet but cannot find him and so grabs Woody instead. Buzz leaps up into the car and is reunited with Woody. A series of gags ensues which result in Woody and Buzz being separated from Andy and the car. There's a neat gag: the Virtual Realty business in the background. Woody and Buzz soon find themselves at Pizza Planet, endeavouring to find Andy, Woody having convinced Buzz that he's secured a spaceship for the ride. The toys are then embroiled in a range of escapades which centre around Buzz thinking that he is at an actual space station.

Also at the Pizza Planet is Andy's nefarious neighbour, Sid, and he kidnaps both Buzz and Woody. The moment of kidnap involves a grabclaw in a booth, a moment which anticipates the grandiose action finale of *Toy Story 3*. Woody and Buzz are then duly imprisoned in Sid's bedroom, a setting rendered in lurid greens and purples that contrast vividly with the primary colours and earthy tones of Andy's room. Commenting on the film's look, Ralph Eggleston explained that, 'We caricatured the sets… Our philosophy for the set indirectly came from Gary Rydstrom, our sound designer and an old friend… he taught me long ago that, in doing sound effects, if a ball bounces, you don't just record the sound of a ball bouncing – because, when the sound effect is cut in, it won't sound like it should. You have to make it bigger.'[73]

In effect, Sid assumes the identity of the mad scientist figure familiar to us from horror movies. Woody and Buzz try to make an escape, but must negotiate Scud, Sid's dog. There's a great character moment when Woody, working through a plan in his mind, taps his fingers together. (Woody runs for freedom saying, 'There's no place like home', a reference to that touchstone of popular film fantasy, *The Wizard of Oz*.) Hands as expressions of thought are key devices in Pixar movies: watch Bob Parr's hand gestures during the office scenes of *The Incredibles*.

Woody discovers under the bed in Sid's room all sorts of freaky, mashed-up toys, the remnants of his former experiments: '…mutant toys, reminiscent of Bosch and Svankmajer and a surprisingly effective foray into existential crisis…'[74] Zombie-like, they are a dark spin on the terrified toys that huddle under the sofa in *Tin Toy*, and surprisingly they come to Woody's aid. As Buzz and Woody make their challenging effort to escape Sid's house of horror, Buzz has an unexpected epiphany when he sees a TV commercial for Buzz Lightyear toys. (Indeed, in *Ratatouille*, it's a TV clip that provides the hero with an epiphany also.) Subsequently, Buzz experiences a massive, momentary depression and identity crisis, and Woody isn't feeling too good either. When Woody eventually calls for the help of his toy friends next door, they momentarily think he has killed Buzz!

As storm clouds gather above usually sunny suburbia, Sid straps a rocket to Buzz to conduct an experiment when the weather clears. Woody tries to brighten Buzz's spirits by explaining that being a toy is all about being cherished. Eventually, Woody and Buzz escape with the help of the 'freakotoys', who gather together to help, an act of community that we also see played out in *Toy Story*'s two sequels, as well as in *A Bug's Life* and *Cars*.

Just as Andy and his mother pull away from home to follow the removal van, Woody and Buzz make a daring, last-minute race and chase to get on board the vehicle where all the other toys have been packed away. Chase sequences work exceptionally well in animation, as *Tom and Jerry* and *Road Runner* attest, and they have formed a key part of cinema's appeal since the earliest days: one has only to watch the stunning Buster Keaton comedy-adventure *The General* to see this manifested.

Using a remote-control car and one of Sid's fireworks, with Buzz attached to it, Woody and Buzz get close to their family, and finally Buzz launches into the air. He and Woody drop down through the sun roof of Andy's mother's car and are safe again. Buzz has accepted himself by story's end. At Christmas in the new house, the toys wait to see what gifts Andy has got. He gets a puppy and the toys are dismayed!

Toy Story, then, is a buddy movie, and buddy movies, as we know, have long been a staple of Hollywood filmmaking. Laurel and Hardy movies are buddy movies, for example, and it's a genre that has long been commercially popular: *Butch Cassidy and the Sundance Kid* (George Roy Hill, 1969), *Lethal Weapon* (Richard Donner, 1987) and *Midnight Run* (Martin Brest, 1988) all attest to the fascination of the scenario in which opposites attract. Think, too, of the friendship of Timothy Mouse and Dumbo in *Dumbo* and of Pinocchio and Jiminy Cricket in *Pinocchio*. 'I've been inspired all my life by Walt Disney films,' John Lasseter has explained, and this acknowledgement, whilst not surprising, is key to understanding how *Toy Story* proved to be such a creative success.

For all of Woody's easygoing, cowboy charm, he has a stampeding selfishness and ego. 'That wasn't flying. That was falling with style,' says Woody to Buzz in an attempt to deflate the spaceman's ego. Of the expressivity of the human face, and its emotional and intellectual resonance, Lasseter explains that 'most of the human emotions are communicated by changes in one or two discrete features.' This subtlety is something that *Toy Story*'s characterisations consistently achieve.

The fantastic premise and situations of *Toy Story* dramatise themes of identity and purpose with humour and invention, and this narrative style continues with *Toy Story 2* and *Toy Story 3*. Certainly, *Toy Story* honours the importance of toys, and hence play, in the imaginative life of children and, as a buddy movie, the film celebrates the coming together of apparently disparate characters who work great as a team. This sense of how the characters value themselves is particularly striking in the second part of the film. Just think about the moment when Buzz's confidence plummets when he realises that he is just a toy. At this point in the story, the adventure that he undertakes is a way for him to determine his value again and that's why his firework flight to freedom with Woody really has an emotional power to it.

Although *Toy Story* is set in the familiar and recognisable location of a child's bedroom in a suburban home, the film creates a somewhat exaggerated design in the presentation of such a well-known locale. Look closely and you'll see that the doors, in their proportions, are a bit taller than they would be in actuality. And the broader visual scheme of the film (along with *Toy Story 2* and *Toy Story 3*) shows the influence of the American illustrator Norman Rockwell. Some people have said quite damningly of Rockwell's work that 'its minute verisimilitude – as well as the exaggeration of every wink, scowl, grin and pout on its characters' faces – had the depthless narrative clarity of TV.'[75] The filmmaker, George Lucas, however, has said in praise of Rockwell that his work displays 'just unfettered emotionalism'.[76] Like Rockwell, Pixar have in many cases constructed very appealing stories about childhood.

As with many genre films, *Toy Story* is enriched further by a musical score performed by an orchestra. It's still perhaps the strangest thing about our relationship with the idea of realism and film that we never seem to object to the presence of such an artificial element in a storytelling process which espouses so strongly the invisibility of technique.

Music and animation, then, have a rich connection, and the lyrical sensibility of both forms makes for this apotheosis. Of the historical link, Mary Ann Skweres writes that 'Music for animation has evolved since its original inception during the silent film era. Although some cartoons may have been delivered to the theatres with "special scores" ...early cartoon music before the age of sync sound focused on the theatre's organ accompaniment as a means to display the musician's wit and skill as opposed to using the music to delineate character or create mood.'[77]

For *Toy Story*, Randy Newman's playful and tender score enriches the drama no end and is by turns sweet and frightening. Newman had established his film music credentials in his Americana-inflected pieces for films including *The Natural* (Barry Levinson, 1984) and *Avalon* (Barry Levinson, 1990). For *Toy Story*, the music is wistful, joyful and necessarily tense as the action requires, and, following the success of *Toy Story*, Newman went on to score *A Bug's Life* (John Lasseter, 1998), *Toy Story 2* (John Lasseter, 2000) and *Monsters, Inc*. Newman's song, 'You've Got A Friend In Me', amusingly and touchingly distils the theme of the film and stylistically echoes the tone of the American vaudeville tradition.

Toy Story, then, defined much of what continues to be considered the typical Pixar style of narrative and visuals. The *Toy Story* trilogy forms a memorably coherent whole in its focus on families and childhood, and also on what an adult might hold most special in their memory of growing up. When *Toy Story* was released, some reviewers in the mainstream press were surprised at the film's accomplishment in so confidently combining technology and aesthetic invention. One verdict was that, 'The characters are as emotionally complex and poignantly sympathetic as those any flesh and blood actors could portray.'[78] Tellingly, many reviewers made a point of flagging up the film's obvious intelligence – '...the major surprise is how much cleverness has been invested in story and dialogue...'[79] – as if this was something you wouldn't generally expect from an animated movie.

Toy Story quickly secured a place for itself as a landmark of animation history, just as *Out of the Inkwell*, *Steamboat Willie*, *Snow White*, *Road Runner*, *Tom and Jerry*, *Mr Magoo* and *Who Framed Roger Rabbit?* before it had done, and the film was duly acknowledged and hailed for successfully fusing technique with storytelling heart. This finely tuned, difficult-to-achieve balance was repeated again with *Toy Story 2* and *Toy Story 3* so that we have a trilogy, an epic of the toy chest, which charts the growth of a great friendship between Woody and Buzz. *Toy Story* is a mesmerising film that balances the spectacle of a new form of computer animation with the accepted conventions of classical storytelling to create a film that is utterly traditional in narrative but very forward looking in technology.

When the film was re-released in 2009, this time in 3D, it continued to entertain, and reviewers were quick to respond to its enduring appeal. Derek Adams in *Time Out* described it as 'so ingenious in concept, design and execution that you could watch it on a postage stamp-sized screen and still be engulfed by its charm.'[80] Andrew Pulver in the *Guardian* wrote that 'its lightness of touch has not diminished, nor has its near-miraculous kidult-fusion humour.'[81]

Thinking about not only this film, but also its two sequels, a quote from the American writer Mark Twain comes to mind regarding the subject of heroism. Twain said that 'One can be a hero to other folk, and in a vague sort of way understand it, or at least believe it, but that a person can really be a hero to a near and familiar friend is a thing which no hero has ever yet been able to realise, I am sure of it.'[82]

A Bug's Life (1998)

Directed by: John Lasseter
Written by: Andrew Stanton, Donald McEnery and Bob Shaw (screenplay), John Lasseter, Joe Ranft and Andrew Stanton (story)
Produced by: Darla K Anderson and Kevin Reher
Music by: Randy Newman
Edited by: Lee Unkrich
Production Design: William Cone

Art Direction: Tia W Kratter and Bob Pauley
Cast: Dave Foley (Flik), Kevin Spacey (Hopper), Julia Louis-Dreyfus (Atta), Hayden Panettiere (Dot), Phyllis Diller (Queen), Richard Kind (Molt), David Hyde Pierce (Slim), Joe Ranft (Heimlich), Denis Leary (Francis), Jonathan Harris (Manny), Madeline Kahn (Gypsy), Bonnie Hunt (Rosie), Michael McShane (Tuck/Roll), John Ratzenberger (PT Flea), Brad Garrett (Dim)

One of the great delights of genre (whether in movies or literature or music) is the fluidity that engulfs and courses through it. And it is this absence of boundaries, in part, which makes for such exciting storytelling opportunities. *A Bug's Life* brightly manifests the delights of these generic fusions, being adventure film, buddy movie, and perhaps even war film.

It's in any creative person or company's interest to have several ideas in development at any one time and *A Bug's Life* was in development at Pixar before *Toy Story* had been released to such massive critical and commercial success.

Looking back now to 1998, we might have the sense that *A Bug's Life* has become, to some extent, the forgotten Pixar film. At the time of the film's release *Toy Story* remained a fresh and well-remembered creative and financial triumph, and *A Bug's Life* was momentarily caught up in the banal and not especially useful discussion about Hollywood's apparent lack of creativity, as evidenced (according to some) by the fact that DreamWorks SKG had near-simultaneously released their first computer-animated film, *Antz*. In reviewing *Antz* for *Sight and Sound* Jonathan Romney wrote: 'Made with digital production house PDI, *Antz* already looks enough of a technical advance on *Toy Story* to cause Lasseter's Pixar company considerable concern. But then, CGI is Hollywood's boom sector – it's awfully competitive out there. [...]The film's range of light effects is considerably more complex than the relatively flat, candy colour palette of *Toy Story*.'[83]

Visually, and tonally, the earliest films produced by DreamWorks Animation and Pixar were highly distinct from each other and, interestingly, in more recent years, Dreamworks Animation's output has become more coherent and dynamic, with particular high points being *Kung Fu Panda* (2008) and *How To Train Your Dragon* (2010). Where *Antz* is a modestly scaled workplace comedy, *A Bug's Life* is an expansive adventure story which confidently asserted Pixar's invention and facility with narrative structure.

As noted elsewhere in this book, Pixar has openly acknowledged the challenges of getting a story 'right' (partly a process of precision and measuring, partly an act of creative alchemy and mystery) in its development phase. Working out the core of any story is a hard creative road.

The original concept for *A Bug's Life* featured a central character called Red who was part of a group of down-on-their-luck circus ants. Inadvertently they become the solution to the ant colony's problems with the grasshoppers. Over a period of six months, storyboards for the film were developed to explore this concept, and this material was just on the verge of becoming the approved story reel for the production to work from when the decision was made to overhaul the entire premise as it seemed too full of storytelling problems. Joe Ranft of Pixar had called it 'stor-re-boarding', a pun that emphasises the process of reworking a concept until it is just right. Certainly, the concept for *A Bug's Life* has the quality of an Aesop's fable about it, being concerned with the diminutive, busy ants working through the summer to prepare for the harsh winter ahead whilst the neighbouring grasshoppers laze around, preparing to reap the rewards of the ants' industry. Of *Aesop's Fables*, the scholar Laura Gibbs has written that, as far back as the first century CE, *Aesop's Fables* 'were put into collections that were used for teaching purposes [...] *Aesop's Fables* were not considered children's literature in the ancient world [...]'[84]

A Bug's Life is effectively an adventure film, a revision of the story which forms the basis of the Akira Kurosawa film, *Seven Samurai* (and John Sturges' *The Magnificent Seven*) in which a village is threatened by marauders, compelling the hapless villagers to recruit more able people to protect their welfare. Like all adventure stories,

A Bug's Life turns on the question asked of its protagonist: are you good enough to accomplish the task at hand? It's a worry we all recognise, probably occurring to most of us at least once a week as we go about our lives at home and at work. In *Hollywood Flatlands*, Esther Leslie brings into the picture the reflections of cultural theorist Walter Benjamin on the meaning of fairy tales, and she notes that, in his work, '[Walter] Benjamin reveals a pedagogical aim. All Mickey Mouse films, in essence, teach audiences about the workings of fear: they do this, as does the Grimm fairy tale, by making them leave home.'[85]

With regard to the film's founding concept, *A Bug's Life* fits right in with a rich and popular tradition of animated movies set in the wild. We can name *Bambi*, *The Lion King* and *Princess Mononoke* as titles of real interest in this respect.

John Lasseter and Andrew Stanton directed *A Bug's Life* working from a story developed by Lasseter, Stanton and Joe Ranft, who had served in the same capacity on *Toy Story*. Ranft had also contributed to storyboard supervision on the very moving *James and the Giant Peach* (Henry Selick, 1996), a film with a similarly expansive, outdoorsy feel of adventure across wild terrain.

Pixar's recognition of the need to revise and amend the screenplay and story of *A Bug's Life* multiple times should encourage all writers never to give themselves a hard time about that aspect of the work. Revising and fixing what you've built with words is a necessary requirement of the creative process. And so the story team and director developed a new concept about a lonely hero who goes and seeks help for his family, and Red became Flik. The circus-ant element of the story at that point remained a part of *A Bug's Life* after the revision. However, a key question that had to be answered by the filmmakers was why the circus troop would stay with the colony when things became rough for them. This was worked through as the story team plotted out the sequence called 'Dot's Rescue' in which a bird attacks the insects and the circus ants inadvertently save Dot and are greeted as the heroes of the hour, and therefore a group to be invited to stick around.

As on all Pixar projects, the film was entirely storyboarded and, in turn, these storyboards became the story reels for the pre-production process (committing the boards to video to get a sense of timing and rhythm). This development period occupied half of the four-year production period. In looking at storyboards for the film one can see how vividly, in pencil form, they express the emotions and dynamic composition that become fully realised in the finished movie.

Typically, we think of a dramatic structure as having three acts, but Stanley Kubrick often talked of feature film narratives comprising six sequences and, for *A Bug's Life*, 26 sequences eventually spanned the film's narrative and some sequences were reconfigured up to 30 times before being approved.

It's fair to say that Pixar's films aren't only appealing because of the characters who inhabit them. They also function so effectively on account of their visual dynamism and a skilfully deployed sense of graphic design. Bill Cone's pastel study of underground light and form for *A Bug's Life* testifies to the creative team's ambition to create a somewhat heightened sense of photorealism that merges the real-looking with a quality that's more painterly. As such, each frame is designed in such a way as to direct our attention to the key information, no matter how busy or detailed the rest of the image is. This fundamental storytelling device has a long tradition in visual art.

In keeping with the studio's fidelity to describing and recreating realities and surfaces that are mostly well known to us, and sometimes less well known, the filmmakers paid close attention to the play of light and shadow at grass-roots level. In turn, a computer programme was written to manufacture the translucency of the world at a bug's-eye level. To quote John Lasseter: 'Imagine being in a world where all the buildings are stained glass – that's what the insect world is like.'[86]

The attention to backlit leaves calls to mind the paintings of American painter Maxfield Parrish who worked in both the nineteenth and twentieth centuries. Noted for his use of the colour lapis lazuli in many of his paintings, his highly recognisable images include *Griselda* (1910) and *Daybreak* (1922). More broadly, this attention to a certain level of realism in recreating the natural world places *A Bug's Life* very much on the continuum of animation and nature that has been a long-running feature of animated films. We might start by recognising a connection, for example, between *A Bug's Life* and the Disney studio's short film *The Old Mill*, and more famously the lyrical allure of Bambi, painted by Tyrus Wong. Of his work on that film, Wong looked to the example of Chinese illustration and also the Barbizon school that engendered Impressionism.

Indeed, the visual riches of the world also feature in *The Incredibles* (2004) and *Up* (2009), and there's something in *Up*'s visual style that marks the affinity Pixar has for the work of Japanese animation company, Studio Ghibli. Then, too, we can also look to the wilderness landscapes conjured in the work of animators Frederick Back and Michel Ocelot. Lasseter and his team decided that they wanted to present the film in CinemaScope format because of the wide vistas, which they wanted to immerse their characters in on their odyssey.

Across Pixar's body of work, a key visual trait has been the photorealism of its lighting and shading effects and impressions. As such, one of the key breakthroughs achieved in the production of *A Bug's Life* was the creation of subdivision surface modelling software, which was a combined effort of the shading and lighting departments to create an illuminating model for transluscent effects and virtual lighting variations. These lighting subtleties enrich the action so that even Dim the beetle has wonderfully iridescent wings, shown in close up as Flik rides back to Ant Island with his supposed warriors.

As with all of Pixar's feature-film projects, the cast of vocal performers for *A Bug's Life* featured actors whose names and voices were very familiar to audiences. As such, the film's star name was Kevin Spacey, voicing the nefarious villain, Hopper. Spacey had become well known just the year before as the devious Keyser Soze in *The Usual Suspects*, and his association in the minds of audiences with cold, aloof characterisations plays its part in the villainy of Hopper. The film's hero, Flik, was voiced by Dave Foley and his high-pitched, youthful tone quickly establishes a necessary sense of fragility that sits in real contrast to the snarling voice of Hopper. Dennis Leary voiced Francis the ladybird and Madeline Kahn was the spider. The identifiable cadences of the actor John Ratzenberger, who features as P T Flea, would also have been recognisable to audiences familiar with his performance as the morose, chronically unlucky Cliff in the sitcom *Cheers*.

A Bug's Life begins on a glorious summertime day. Ant Island is a bucolic haven for an efficiently run colony of ants which we watch going about their daily lives. Complicating their admirably efficient routine is the need to preserve their safety by gathering a food offering for the grasshoppers who protect the ants from other, larger bugs.

One of the ants, a young male named Flik, is rather clumsy and, in due course, this clumsiness causes the food offering to topple just when the grasshoppers turn up for their store. The grasshoppers attack and threaten the colony and Flik is duly put before the Queen and her council. This encounter between youth and the collective authorities also features in the Pixar film *Cars* (2006). Flik offers to go and find help in fighting off the grasshoppers, leaving the ants to gather food before the start of autumn.

Flik undertakes his mission and ventures to the city, a rubbish pile near a trailer and car. Performing in a makeshift tent is the bug circus of P T Flea, most definitely not entertaining the scant audience at all, despite their best efforts. Flik is just thinking he will never find other, bigger bugs who are happy to help when he enters a bar and sees the circus troupe striking a suitably heroic pose. The bugs think Flik is a talent scout and readily follow him when he expresses interest. Flik is flown back to Ant Island and, en route, tells them more about his mission.

Back at Ant Island, the bugs finally understand what it is they have really been recruited for and make a quick departure. Flik is unable to convince them to stay and ventures out beyond the cover of the island. Dot, the youngest daughter of the Ant Queen and friend of Flik, follows him and is attacked by a bird. Flik and the bugs ride to the rescue and return to Ant Island as heroes.

The Ant Princess makes Flik the liaison between ants and bugs and, in thinking about how to defeat Hopper, a plan is hatched to create a fake bird to scare him away for good. The ants and bugs work together.

Meanwhile, Hopper and his cronies are getting eager to return to Ant Island, especially when Hopper reminds them that the ants could easily overthrow them because of their sheer numbers.

At Ant Island, the circus bugs are now part of life but, at the critical moment, P T Flea turns up looking for his actors. Only now do the ants realise the true identity of the presumed warrior bugs. Appearances can be deceptive. Flik is banished for lying to the colony and leaves with the bugs.

The last leaf of summer falls and the grasshoppers arrive at Ant Island. Dot and her friends hide and Dot learns that Hopper wants to wipe out the Ant Queen. She flies to tell Flik and convinces him to return. A plan is hatched and the ants fight back with the help of the bugs and the model bird. Flik confronts Hopper, who savagely attacks him. Finally, the ants mob the grasshoppers and Hopper is caught by a real bird.

Order returns to the colony and the circus bugs depart. Flik, Dot and the Princess look proudly over the colony as another summer begins.

Like *Toy Story*, *A Bug's Life* sustains an energetic rhythm and exercises real control of tone, moving with ease from moments of humour to moments of jeopardy and tension, and often combining both. The characters of *A Bug's Life* cover all the archetypes necessary to represent the good, the bad and the ugly of human behaviour. The good bugs are all young people, who, in times of need, turn to their elders for guidance. Dot is a supercute supporting character who just wants to fly. Princess Atta is a strong-willed young woman who is just as afraid of getting things wrong as Flik is.

Flik occupies the role of the classic young hero, who, like so many before him, and many after him, must find his place in the world and, in true heroic fashion, get out beyond the safe confines of home in order to undertake an adventure that draws out his best nature. As we acknowledged in the introduction to this book, the hero of the ancient wonder tales was often the object of others' scorn and ridicule and would then eventually rise to success and happiness. Flik's adventure ultimately sees him return home to his community with a gift that will benefit everyone. Flik even finds it in himself to stand up to the bullying Hopper and also to generate a little romance with Princess Atta. We might say that it is Flik's capacity to dream and also to imagine that the colony can save itself which propels him forward, serving as the power that will help him win the day. Throughout most of the film Flik regards himself as a clumsy failure (a feeling we can all relate to), but ultimately redeems himself through his thoughts and acts of courage and bravery.

In vivid contrast to Flik's goodness and the unthreatening nature of his appearance is his nemesis, Hopper. This scarred grasshopper is the unrepentant villain of the film, his tendency to savagery marked by the scar just below his right eye. For sure, his angular exoskeleton is very armour-like in contrast to the rounded forms of the ants. Hopper is more than just bullying the ants for food – he is driven by the fear that the grasshopper way of life could be eradicated if the ants ever realised just how much they outnumbered the grasshoppers.

Counterpointing the brooding villainy of Hopper and his tribe are the circus bugs, who most vividly provide the film with its comedy. Each of the circus bugs is vividly characterised, and all of them are desperate for approval and a sense of belonging. Like Flik, they too realise their potential and find a place in the world. *A Bug's Life* confidently combines scenes of menace and jeopardy with scenes of energy. The most spooky element of the film is the crazed ant who is kept on a chain and who pursues Dot late in the story. The film ably spoofs and honours the conventions of the adventure genre and also features a level of violence that is a little more intense than any to be found in the other Pixar films.

A Bug's Life was a hugely successful release, assuring both audiences and Pixar that *Toy Story* was not a creative or commercial fluke. It was also John Lasseter's second feature film as director and, with this film, he contributed to the interesting tension between studio identity and director as author in their own right. Of this relationship, historically, animation historian Maureen Furniss has noted that 'as the film industry grew, production became much more complex, making it increasingly difficult for directors and other artists to retain creative control over their work'.[87]

Looking back to 1998, we can see the rapidly emerging fascination with, and growing veneration of, Pixar as something of a saviour of the American animated feature film. By this time, Disney's renaissance period of *The Little Mermaid* (Ron Musker, 1989) through to *The Lion King* had been and gone and computer-animated characters (albeit rendered photorealistically and called 'visual effects' in live-action films) had really begun to make their mark in films such as *Terminator 2: Judgement Day* (1991), *Jurassic Park* and *Jumanji* (1995). By the early years of the twenty-first century, as digital animation embedded itself, moving from visual novelty to legitimate stylistic choice, the cel animation that had characterised the Disney rebirth, and which had become increasingly expensive, quickly declined as a commercially viable production format. It's correct, too, however, to note that cel animation continues to be very present in European and east Asian animation industries, as movies such as *The Illusionist* (2006) and *Arrietty* (2012) show.

Narratively and visually (both inextricably connected, of course) *A Bug's Life* was more expansive, intricate (in plot and design) and busier in action than *Toy Story*. Both films are bound together by their diminutive heroes, a feature that also characterises *Finding Nemo* (2003) and *Ratatouille*. Is it any wonder that children enjoy these stories?

The ant colony is very much set in its ways and must learn to think afresh in order to defeat its oppressive enemy. Could it be that this is an example of pop culture reaching for the tone of a political film in the broadest and best sense?

'You have rekindled the long dormant embers of purpose in our lives.' (Manty to Flik)

'It's a bug eat bug world out there.' (Hopper to the ants)

Of popular culture, Chris Barker has written that its value lies in expressing popular meanings and values at a given time, and perhaps also – and this is the telling bit in all of this – that popular culture gives a voice to those otherwise without power or influence. Pop culture, then, is empowering.[88]

All films are political and ideological in that they each construct a view of the world and a way of functioning in it, and we might say that, with *A Bug's Life*, Pixar established the political subtext of its films. This does not mean party political but instead something more rounded and, in fact, philosophical: a worldview, if you like. All films communicate and, somewhat dangerously, entertainment is considered a diversion from anything 'meaningful'. As such, it can actually do very much the opposite, the label entertainment distracting people from the smuggling of ideas into the story.

The film brilliantly conjures the heat and bright light of summer and, similarly, the pinks and cooler colours of autumnal mornings. Just watch the scene where the grasshoppers race in at summer's end to get the food from Ant Island.

The film's opening moments do something akin to the opening moments of *Snow White* (1937), which is that they replicate the natural world with real subtlety so that the first image is of the blazing sun and flares. The camera then reveals water before gently pushing in softly on a tree swaying in a summer breeze. The camera moves through the grass and, in the sharply focused midground, ants appear. The foreground and background blades are out of focus. As with *Toy Story* and *Monsters, Inc*, *A Bug's Life* brims with kinetic energy and delicate facial animation. Just look at Flik's forlorn face throughout the film, especially as he sits in the back of P T Flea's wagon towards the end of the story. A standout sequence in the film is the bird attack on Dot where the bird screeches and roars, rather like the velociraptors in *Jurassic Park*, making the link between birds and their prehistoric predecessors. Both films share the same sound designer, Gary Rydstrom, who has said of the role of sound in film that 'there's nothing as interesting as a real sound effect'.

As in all of Pixar's films, visual comedy is abundant in *A Bug's Life*, notably in the set-piece scene that introduces the hapless circus troupe at work. *A Bug's Life* has a discernible sense of action and comedy influenced by Tex Avery and also by the live-action traditions of silent film comedy. Contrast this energy with the more violent action of Hopper towards the ants at the end of the film, such as when he slams his foot down on Flik, bruised and bloodied by his confrontation.

It's always been one of the pleasures of animation to see how it concocts miniature versions of the human-scaled and orientated world. *A Bug's Life* maxes out on this – in this film, bug versions of human stuff, notably Flik's leafy baseball cap and the raindrop telescope. In the bar scene there is even a mosquito who drinks a Bloody Mary and then explodes in an intentional, or otherwise, reference to Winsor McCay exploding a mosquito in his animated short, *How A Mosquito Operates* (1911). On 15 September 2012, Google celebrated McCay's birthday with a charming Google graphic that riffed on his *Little Nemo in Slumberland* comic strip.

Watching *A Bug's Life* one is reminded, too, of how Randy Newman's music has become the sound of Pixar, rather like Carl Stalling's was identified with Bugs Bunny cartoons and other Warner Brothers shorts, Danny Elfman's became the soundtrack of Tim Burton's films, John Williams's the sound of a Steven Spielberg film, and Bernard Herrmann's music an integral part of an Alfred Hitchcock movie. Newman's music for *A Bug's Life* can be characterised as being suitably epic in scale, suggesting the influence of composer Elmer Bernstein, who scored *The Magnificent Seven*. For the action sequences of *A Bug's Life* the music is seriously melodramatic and intense and, when Flik arrives in the city, Newman easily parodies the style of composer George Gershwin, whose great achievements included the opera *Porgy and Bess*.

When *A Bug's Life* was released in autumn 1998, computer-animated features were still very much an emerging format and films were still being produced in America using cel animation, notably the elegant and affecting *The Prince of Egypt*. *A Bug's*

Life further suggested the commercial appeal of the computer-animated film, and soon it became the norm and not the 'novelty' exception. It's now the case that a hand-drawn animated film would be the novelty, in the American studio system at least; cel-produced movies continue to be made around the world.

Roger Ebert once commented that 'animation contains enormous promise for a new kind of storytelling, freed from reality and gravity, but although the Japanese have exploited that freedom, too many American feature cartoons follow the Disney formula of plucky young heroes and heroines and comic sidekicks'.[89]

In Britain, the magazine *Sight and Sound* noted that 'the film has fun mixing bug-world givens with anthropomorphism'.[90] *Time Out* magazine observed that 'the computer generated imagery [...] is exceptional throughout'.[91]

With its wide vistas and epic adventure narrative, *A Bug's Life* differs significantly from the more enclosed world of *Toy Story* and *Monsters, Inc* and anticipates the aquatic quest and oceanic expanse/images of *Finding Nemo*.

The film celebrates the value of community and good faith in one another as a means to salvation and harmony, and this is a perspective that also shines through in *Toy Story 2* and *Toy Story 3*. This is a left-leaning movie that says we're all in this together. Like Dumbo, Flik comes to realise his own potential in part through his own shortcomings. It is his eagerness to please that sets him on his journey out into the world, returning like a real hero to save his own world, in doing so continuing the tradition of the ancient-wonder-tale format. Flik is nothing less than the enduring, oft-mocked young man who eventually proves everyone around him wrong when he is the one who goes right ahead and accomplishes great things. It's certainly a story that bears repeating, and heeding, no matter how old we get. What apparently held Flik down only serves to take him up.

Toy Story 2 (1999)

Directed by: John Lasseter; Co-Directors: Ash Brannon and Lee Unkrich
Written by: Chris Webb, Doug Chamberlin and Rita Hsaio, Andrew Stanton (screenplay); Andrew Stanton, John Lasseter, Pete Docter, Ash Brannon (story)
Produced by: Karen Robert Jackson and Sarah McArthur
Music by: Randy Newman
Edited by: Edie Bleiman, David Ian Salter and Lee Unkrich
Cast: Tom Hanks (Woody Pride), Tim Allen (Buzz Lightyear), Joan Cusack (Jessie), Kelsey Grammer (Stinky Pete), Wayne Knight (Al), John Ratzenberger (Hamm), Jim Varney (Slinky), Laurie Metcalf (Mum)

After several decades in which we've seen produced a number of rather brilliant sequels to already rather marvellous originals, there remains a somewhat narrow-minded, knee-jerk reaction that still tends to say that movie sequels are a sign of creative bankruptcy, with the film industry needing to sell product that is recognisable. Of course, as an industry, this is one of its first, foremost, and most obvious, commitments. That doesn't mean, however, that a product cannot be inventive and articulate as well. A sequel might even surpass the original film's ambitions, and also its creative success in the way that it creates engaging characters, environments and dramatic situations ranging from slapstick comedy through to the height of melodrama and the depths of tragedy. *The Godfather Part II* (Francis Ford Coppola, 1974) and *The Empire Strikes Back* (Irvin Kershner, 1980) are typically referenced in this regard and we can also add to the roster of sequels that provide their own rewarding pleasures: *Back to the Future Part II* (Robert Zemeckis, 1989), the *Three Colours* trilogy (Krzysztof Kieslowski, 1993–4) and the *Apu* trilogy (Satyajit Ray, 1955–9).

Of sequels, David Bordwell has commented that not all are automatically bereft of interest or value: 'Most film industries need to both standardise and differentiate their products. Audiences expect a new take on some familiar forms and materials. Sequels offer the possibility of recognisable repetition with controlled, sometimes intriguing variation. This logic can be found in sequels in other media, which often respond to popular demand for the same again, but different.'[92]

Toy Story 2 has the same self-referential brilliance as *Back to the Future Part II* (in many ways, that film is even better than the original) and we might say that *Toy Story 2* is arguably more emotionally rich and satisfying than the original *Toy Story* feature. In order to reach this satisfactory outcome, however, the production of the film proved somewhat fraught.

Perhaps surprisingly, given the immense success of *Toy Story*, the sequel was originally going to be only a direct-to-video release, something which had proven to be an extremely productive profit centre for Disney. However, when the Disney studio reviewed the film's story reel (typically, hand-drawn storyboards supplemented by audio of the dialogue proposed for each shot/scene) they committed to releasing it theatrically, investing more money and resources into the project. Subsequently, certain changes had to be made to the narrative based on this expansion process.

Of *Toy Story 2* Lasseter acutely observed that, 'One of the things that's different about this film is that it's one of the rare times that a sequel actually changes genre from the original.'[93]

As the maxim goes: writing is rewriting, and in filmmaking it's just as true, *Toy Story* underwent intensive revisions. The rethinking, and refining, of a concept way ahead of the expensive business of realising it as moving images is vital. And so it was that, in the autumn of 1998, significantly deep into the production phase on *Toy Story 2*, John Lasseter made a decision. To his mind the film was not shaping up, so he halted production and presented the crew with the revised story they would now have the job of realising, in just seven short months, as a movie.

Certainly, the quality of this particular sequel is enhanced by the return of the original cast, rounded out by the new performers Kelsey Grammer as Stinky Pete, Joan Cusack as Jessie and Wayne Knight as the neurotic, obsessive toy merchant, Al.

As part of the evolutionary process of filmmaking, many of the production process lessons learned on *Toy Story* and *A Bug's Life* were developed and refined on *Toy Story 2*. Of the film's elaborately designed, very amusing prologue, a space-set showdown between Zurg and Buzz, John Lasseter described it as '*Star Wars* simmered for a long time and boiled down to a nice, rich sauce.'[94] The allusion is accurate and speaks of the skill with which Pixar has often found a point of reference in film history and refashioned it for their own purposes. This speaks of a healthy cultural capital on the part of the studio, an awareness that no story exists in a vacuum.

One of the benefits of computer-based work is easy access to archives of material. Thus, the production could use trees and leaves that had previously been created for *A Bug's Life*. The Pixar team also developed a more sophisticated virtual camera style for this film and a year was spent in research and development, refining approaches to lighting and shading of the settings and characters.

Toy Story 2 built on the original film's aesthetic, refining its fidelity to visual realism. For example, in the shots of Woody's old-time TV show the image was given 20 layers of fake degradation. And just look at how they've been able to backlight suburban trees. Critical to the narrative logic, the film would also differ from the original by approaching the action from both human and toy perspectives.

Toy Story 2 begins in space, metallic-looking opening titles rushing towards us, in the spirit of *Superman: The Movie* (Richard Donner, 1978). There's a little bit of parody going on here for sure as the orchestral score thunderously adds to the sense of scale. Rocketing into view is Buzz Lightyear as he descends towards a planet and rushes through a canyon, and is then surrounded by countless bad-guy robots. He dispatches them and then finds himself underground approaching his nemesis Zurg, or rather the (amusing) power that drives him. We then get a reality check and the action cuts and we're back in Andy's bedroom once more with the toys playing. This story-within-a-story prologue is an expansion of what we see at points in *Toy Story* and it certainly anticipates what we see in *Toy Story 3* with its Western-styled prologue sequence. There's knowing delight laced throughout this material.

Woody is, as in *Toy Story* and *Toy Story 3*, a little anxious and concerned about the prospect of change, even if it's of the good sort. Andy is heading to Cowboy Camp and he's going to take Woody with him, and so Woody gathers his fellow toys together to brief them about what will be happening during his short absence. Having attended to this day-to-day business, Woody restates the connection he feels to Andy when he says of Cowboy Camp that 'it's the one time when it's just me and Andy'.

The action then introduces into the story structure what will emerge as the critical plot device as the toys catch a commercial on TV for a toy shop called Al's Toy Barn. The toys freak out slightly and turn the channel over, but not before making a mental note of Al being dressed as a chicken. Andy then comes into the room, the toys freeze and Andy plays with them. As he does so there's a close-up, emphasising the importance of it to the plot, of Woody's arm as it tears at the seam. Andy suddenly doesn't want to take a broken toy to camp and so Woody gets put up on the bookshelf. In this moment, Woody's expression really does resemble his face as sketched by Pixar artist Bud Luckey in a conceptual drawing made during development work on the original *Toy Story*. The camera pulls slowly away from Woody up on the shelf, the move reinforcing his newfound loneliness.

The next day Andy returns early from camp and then immediately drops Woody when he remembers that he has a broken arm. Woody falls in slow motion… into a deck of cards… and then a bin from out of which emerges a mega-zombie-toy beast. Andy looks down at Woody as though looking down into a well. We are in Woody's dreamscape, Woody is relieved to realise. Interestingly, though, each *Toy Story* film includes a nightmarish moment of this kind.

Reality having kicked back in for Woody, it turns out to be not much better than the dream: Andy's mum is preparing a yard sale and the toys freak out. Andy's mother gathers up several toys from Andy's bedroom (Rex's panicked expression as her hand passes close by is very amusing) but none of the main characters gets taken. However, a little, hidden-away toy named Wheezy does get taken for the sale and, as Woody watches him go, the moment is tinged with a sense of mortality. Woody promptly calls Buster the dog to ride him to Wheezy's rescue and, sure enough, Woody accomplishes his mission but, in doing so, he himself is imperilled. As several chance instances unfold in the space of a moment (as they do in *Toy Story* and *Toy Story 3*), each leading to an increased level of jeopardy for Woody, calamity ensues when Woody is stolen by a middle-aged man attending the yard sale. The man is Al, the proprietor of the Toy Barn. The other toys watch somewhat helplessly as Woody is taken away by Al! Buzz immediately recognises that it's time to rescue their good friend and pursues Al's car, mistakes a registration plate for a secret code but then, with the help of Speak and Spell back in Andy's room, works out where the car is heading.

The action cuts to Woody who nows finds himself, like Nemo in *Finding Nemo*, imprisoned behind glass. Woody is in Al's apartment and he immediately tries to escape, realising that he is in the big city, far from the comforts of suburbia. Whilst attempting his seemingly futile escape, Woody meets Jessie, the toy cowgirl Al also has safely boxed away. And so begins, for Woody, an experience equivalent to the one Buzz had in *Toy Story*: a bit of an identity crisis. Woody is then introduced to Jessie's friend, Stinky Pete, and they happily refer to Woody as the prodigal son, to his unease. They explain that they, along with Bullseye the horse, have been waiting for Woody so that they can become a complete collectible toy set that can be sold to a toy museum in Japan. Woody is not impressed by this scenario and is even more compelled to get home. Woody then sees that in Al's apartment there is a virtual shrine to Woody's 1950s mass popularity: toys, collectibles and books fill a wall, all bathed in a somewhat golden light. Woody suddenly understands his origins. Al then arrives home and approaches Woody, who then tears his already frayed arm right off.

The action then cuts back to suburbia as Buzz leads the toys out on the beginning of their quest to rescue Woody. Back at Al's apartment, Woody tries to recover his arm from Al as he sleeps, a moment rather recalling Jack going to recover the gold from the sleeping giant in *Jack and the Beanstalk*. Out in the world, Buzz and the toys close in on Woody and, meanwhile, in Al's apartment, Woody's arm is fixed by an old man who some will recognise as Geri from the Pixar short, *Geri's Game* (Jan Pinkava, 1998).

In Al's Toy Barn, Buzz and the toys encounter dozens of Buzz Lightyear toys on the shelves. Al is then called by the museum and the ticking clock of the plot kicks in as the museum dictate a timeframe within which they want to have the toys flown over. Woody and Jessie's relationship becomes worse as she wants him to stay, but Woody explains that he wants to return home to Andy. Woody goes to make up with Jessie and it's clear that she understands very much how he feels about wanting to get home when she says, 'You feel like you're alive 'cos that's how he sees you.' She then explains her own story through song as we see her life with 'her' child, Emily, who eventually abandons her. The *Toy Story* films are all about accepting change and the images accompanying 'Jessie's Song' conclude with a shot of a sunset. Woody looks saddened by the story; then he goes to the vent that is his escape route. However, Stinky Pete intervenes, preventing Woody's escape, and the old man makes a comment that might sound right at home in *Peter Pan*: 'Andy's grown up and there's nothing you can do about it. You can stay with us and last forever.'

The action then cuts from Woody's low point to Buzz and the toys as they get ever closer to their friend, negotiating their own series of comical and complicated sidetracks along the way. In Al's apartment, Woody has a change of heart and expresses his excitement at going to the museum in Japan where he will never fall out of favour with the adoring children visiting him there. At that moment his friends arrive to free him and he explains that he wants to go to Japan. Buzz is not pleased by this and there's a neat reversal here of a memorable moment in *Toy Story*: this time it's Buzz who insists to Woody: 'You... are... a... toy!' Buzz then proceeds to remind Woody that 'life's only worth living if you're being loved by a kid'. In a way, the toys see themselves as parental figures to the children, unassumingly looking out for them.

Woody insists that he won't come back to Andy's and so the toys leave him with Jessie and Pete. As Buzz leads the gang back down the shaft for the journey home he looks forlorn as he hears Woody singing 'You've Got A Friend In Me' on the TV.

As with *Up*, though, it's the power of memory that provides Woody with his point of no return. The cowboy looks down at the freshly repainted sole of his boot and wipes the paint away to reveal the name 'Andy'. He remembers, and he knows that he must go home, even if that does mean seeing Andy grow up and move on with his life eventually. Woody says that Jessie, the horse and Pete should go with him. Just as he begins to feel his spirits revive, Woody is challenged by Stinky Pete who now reveals his true feelings and prevents Woody from escaping as this would jeopardise the prospect of a new life in Japan. Al then comes in and packs everything up for the plane trip. The film moves into its final act as Woody, Jessie and Pete are taken to the airport for loading onto the plane. Buzz and company ride to the rescue in classic Western style and Woody and Jessie are rescued just in time. Pete has a different fate. We then see all of the toys back home in Andy's bedroom with Jessie now a part of the family. Order has been restored and lessons have again been learned.

'Jessie's Song' is one of the highlights of the film and harks back to the tradition of the movie musical, one which Pixar initially shunned and have, for the most part, continued to avoid. Here's film scholar Richard Dyer on the relationship between musicals and entertainment, and his comment seems entirely fitting in relation to Pixar's films: 'Entertainment does not [...] present models of utopian worlds [...] Rather the utopianism is contained in the feelings it embodies. It presents [...] what utopia would feel like rather than how it would be organised.'[95]

In considering 'Jessie's Song' we can also bring into play a reference to the animation specialist Ed Hooks who says of memory being expressed in animation that 'understanding the way memory works is important to animators because there is a particular kind of expression on the face of a person who is remembering something'[96]. Hooks adds that, in cinema, 'a scene is a negotiation'. As such, 'Jessie's Song' provides a variation on this function.[97]

Reviews of *Toy Story 2* were, for the most part, hugely ecstatic. Roger Ebert wrote of the film that 'The movie once again features the enchanting three-dimensional feel of computer-generated animation by Pixar...'[98] Other critics described it as 'a sequel that takes chances and hits pay dirt with emotional nuances and riotous satire'[99] and 'an extremely sophisticated, surprisingly melancholy understanding of the importance, resonance and tragically brief shelf life of the average plaything'[100].

In its focus on the power of change and the role of memory, *Toy Story 2* anticipates a large swathe of Pixar's subsequent productions, and the film perhaps continues to set the bar for what Pixar can achieve in terms of film sequels and the possibilities they offer to enrich the characters introduced in an original title.

Monsters, Inc (2001)

Directed by: Pete Docter, David Silverman, Lee Unkrich
Written by: Robert L Baird, Jill Culton, Pete Docter, Dan Gerson, Jeff Pidgeon, Rhett Reese, Jonathan Roberts, Andrew Stanton
Produced by: Darla K Anderson
Executive Producer: John Lasseter
Associate Producer: Kori Rae
Music by: Randy Newman
Sound by: Tom Myers
Edited by: James Austin Stewart
Production Design: Harley Jessup, Bob Pauley
Art Direction: Tia W Kratter, Dominique Louis
Animators: Angus MacLane, Dave Mullins
Cast: John Goodman (Sulley), Billy Crystal (Mike Wazowski), Mary Gibbs (Boo), Steve Buscemi (Randall Boggs), James Coburn (Henry J Waternoose III), Jennifer Tilly (Celia), Bob Peterson (Roz), John Ratzenberger (Yeti), Frank Oz (Fungus), Dan Gerson (Needleman/

Smitty), Steve Susskind (Floor Manager), Bonnie Hunt (Flint), Jeff Pidgeon (Bile), Sam Penguin Black (George Sanderson)

'We scare, because we care.' That is the mantra of the Monsters, Inc company and it alerts us also to the film's aim of inverting our expectations, of giving us an alternative view on familiar things. After all, stories play their part in our lives and, at their best, should always offer a new perspective. Of monsters and ghouls and the fascination they have for us, Marina Warner wrote that:

> The theory that children need to compensate for their own hapless dependence by imagining themselves huge and powerful and cruel has also normalised all manner of frightening play acting, equating children with monsters, childhood with a savage state. Stephen Jay Gould, the biologist, has pointed out that kids don't have an innate kinship with dinosaurs, but that it has been fostered by intensive marketing; the relationship seems based in some idea of shared primitiveness – and future extinction. Lots of toys appeal to the idea of children's savagery: from huge furry, clawed slippers for tiny tots to wear to bed to warn off any other beasts in the night, to dinosaur lunchboxes and watches. As a gift catalogue describes, 'At the touch of a button, the fearsome tyrannosaurus rex emits a blood-curdling little roar.' In the very midst of consecrating innocence, the modern mythology of childhood ascribes to children a specially rampant natural appetite for all kinds of transgressive pleasures, including above all the sado-masochistic thrills of fear. And these child heroes – and heroines – now enjoy a monopoly on all kinds of unruly passions which adults later have to learn to control in themselves.[101]

Maybe the folks at Pixar read Marina Warner, maybe they don't, but that's not the point. The point is that many films trigger something deep and ancient in us regarding what might scare us, prompting us to make the connections with our own experience of life and with other narratives, whether they're movies, songs, books, comics or computer games.

Most of the time, any film that involves monsters tends to be either a science-fiction or a horror film. With *Monsters, Inc* the genre in which the monsters are found is a comedy. Before we go any further, though, let's just stop and consider an influence on Pixar that seems not to get widely enough recognised. I'm referring here to the impact of puppeteer, film director and producer Jim Henson. Pete Docter's Pixar films, more than any other from the studio, seem to me to have qualities redolent of the Henson vibe in their playfulness and, more importantly, their open-heartedness.

Most famously, Jim Henson was the creator of *The Muppets* and, of course, the puppetry and animation connection is a long-standing and rich one. Henson achieved the rare and wondrous balancing act of being totally fantastical whilst still managing to make a sincere connection with well-understood, long-held human truths. Like animation, puppetry is a useful means by which to smuggle in a subversive, serious idea, whilst never letting the audience feel patronised or bludgeoned with 'meaning'.

Henson's legacy, then, continues. Indeed, during his working life, he showed the ways in which puppetry and animation were two sides of the same creative coin, producing upbeat fantasies that reached out to a popular audience. Through Henson we can trace a link back to Walt Disney and Winsor McCay, and then further back beyond that to the traditions of puppetry he tapped into, and which so much animation has its roots in. As an exercise in comparison and contrast watch Tim Burton's highly entertaining, 'painterly' adaptation of *Alice in Wonderland* (2010) alongside the Henson-infused *Dreamchild* (Gavin Lambert, 1985).

Henson's output, then, brought animation (and visual effects) into a sweet dance with puppetry, the longer-term conjuring trick manifesting itself in today's hit fantasy films. I think there's a point to be made here too, however, about a potential difference between contemporary fantasy and the fantasy cinema and television Henson produced. Where today's live action and animated fantasy fusions tend to go for the brooding, and sometimes just plain morose, there's a real joyfulness, playfulness and recognition of the value of silliness in Henson's work that is very appealing. Furthermore, the puppet characters populating Henson's work as director and producer serve as a useful frame of reference for animators in terms of crafting a performance, with all the inherent issues of timing and pacing. Henson knew how to fabricate connections between setting and character in the creation of stories that resonated with a real kind of emotional and psychological relevance. His films and TV programmes celebrate community, and he seemed to be perceptive about the power of the fairy tale.

Henson said of his work that, 'My hope still is to leave the world a bit better than when I got here.'[102] Certainly, there are many who would agree that he did.

As with many initial concepts abandoned in the development process of a creative project, one of the early notions for the premise of *Monsters, Inc* sounds fascinating. A 30-year-old man is given a childhood book by his mother. Inside the book are a cluster of drawings he had made as a kid of monsters. These images come to life and play havoc with the grown man's working and romantic life. Ultimately, the man confronts his fears with the help of the monsters. This idea was seen as lacking in one critical area, namely an absence of any child at the heart of the story. The concept which eventually developed into the film as we know it was based on exploring the theme of fear, a subject common to both children and young people. Bruno Bettelheim has written that, 'There are fairy tales which tell about the need to be able to feel fear. A hero may survive hair-raising adventures without any anxiety, but he can find satisfaction in life only after the ability to feel fear is restored to him.'[103]

For director Pete Docter, for whom *Monsters, Inc* was his feature directing debut, the notion of monsters functioning as the basis for a film story began to develop during the production of *A Bug's Life*. Just as being toys was a job for the toys in *Toy Story*, the monsters' job was to be monstrous. The characters are ordinary working-class heroes and the film's interest in monsters – and therefore the tricks our imaginations play on us about monsters hiding in the cupboard – perhaps anticipates an aspect of Pete

Docter's forthcoming third directorial project, which will explore the workings of the human mind.

The first 18 months of *Monsters, Inc*'s production period were spent developing the concept and narrative, and it was John Lasseter who suggested that maybe the monsters should be scared of the children they are meant to be scaring. A critical balance had to be found between scary monsters and non-scary monsters. All the monster body shapes were fairly rounded which immediately minimised the sense of threat. Deleted scenes included one of Sulley making a scare and being more afraid of the child than the child is of him. At this stage in story development he was only an assistant scary monster. Indeed, if you look at a Sulley character design by Geefwee Boedoe, you'll see Sulley caught in a spotlight. He has big horns, tentacles and no legs, and looks less ursine and more like a generic monster.

Unsurprisingly, realising a design that worked for the character of Sulley was a challenge. Intriguingly, one of the earliest sketches for the character, rendered with marker pen, remains very evident in the full, final design. In his first iteration he was a clumsy, scary monster. He always had fur, though, and llama fur was used as the key reference for his movement and appearance.

Characteristically, the settings for the action of *Monsters, Inc* are replete with details and invention. For example, a local gas refinery inspired the look of the Monsters, Inc base, which is a huge sprawling factory. If you look through other conceptual drawings for the world in which *Monsters, Inc* is situated we can describe it as being American-urban in its style, but with a more European flourish in part, too.

As with other Pixar films, the characters were brought to life vocally by a number of recognisable actors familiar to audiences from film and TV. For Sulley, the actor John Goodman was engaged, and his warm, deep voice fits perfectly with the large, lumbering form of the character. Goodman had done similarly strong vocal work in the relatively little-seen animated feature *We're Back!* (Ralph and Dick Zondag, 1993), for which he voiced a far-from-threatening

Tyrannosaurus Rex who finds himself transported to modern-day New York. Over his long career, Goodman's onscreen persona has tended towards strong, vivid characters and, on account of his large frame, a sense of security comes with that. Goodman had broken through with his starring role in the American sitcom *Roseanne*, after which he began featuring in movies, notably *Raising Arizona* (Joel Coen, 1987), *Sea of Love* (Harold Becker, 1989), *Always* (Steven Spielberg, 1989) and *Barton Fink* (Joel Coen, 1990). Of his involvement with *Monsters, Inc* Goodman made an interesting point about vocal work in terms of it relating to his own past when he said, 'I listened to a lot of radio theatre when I was a kid and I've always been a fan of that stuff.'[104]

Sulley's best buddy is Mike, who is the physical opposite of Sulley. The film plays, like *Toy Story*, on the buddy-movie format, and this characterises *Up* and *Finding Nemo* also. Comedian and comedy movie star Billy Crystal performed the character of the neurotic, wisecracking Mike. Crystal has been a movie staple since the late 1980s when he appeared in *Throw Momma From the Train* (Danny DeVito, 1988), *When Harry Met Sally* (Rob Reiner, 1989), *Mr Saturday Night* (Billy Crystal, 1991) and *Analyze This* (Harold Ramis, 1998). Of Crystal's movie persona, channelled neatly into Mike, we can say that it is nervy and high energy. Billy Crystal and John Goodman recorded their dialogue together, a relatively unusual practice but one which allows for an authentic interaction between the characters. The accepted character drawings were sculpted by Jerome Ranft into clay maquettes. Full-sized heads were also sculpted and these were marked with grids so that they could be scanned into the computer as references.

For the film's villains, two rich vocal performances were obtained from James Coburn as Waternoose and Steve Buscemi as conniving Randall Boggs, slimy of voice and sleazily slinky of move. Buscemi has appeared in *Reservoir Dogs* (Quentin Tarantino, 1992), *Trees Lounge* (Steve Buscemi, 1996), *Armageddon* (Michael Bay, 1999) and the little-known movie *Monster House* (Gil Kenan, 2006), one of the very best examples of performance-capture filmmaking.

One of the first creative steps in the process of developing the right story and tone of delivery for *Monsters, Inc* was to develop a colour script, which is a document comprising postage-stamp-sized pastel thumbnails showing the dominant colour scheme of each scene. It's an element used not just for Pixar films but, typically, on most animated film productions – and live action too – giving a sense of the visual mood for each sequence. Viewed as a whole, a colour script functions as an easy-to-read map of an entire film's colour scheme and hence some guide to the moods being presented. Specific sequences will then be storyboarded and, on *Monsters, Inc*, these initial concept art images informed the shape of the screenplay as it was drafted by Andrew Stanton and Dan Gerson.

Director Pete Docter explained that 'the overall design philosophy for Monstropolis was to think of it as our world – only monsters live there'.[105] For example, the individual work stations in the factory area where the doors appear were modelled in part after a classic bowling alley, and the idea was that the factory had been built in the early 1960s so as to maximise the opportunities for spooking during the Baby Boom-era (1945–50) during which the birth rate in North America and Europe spiked after World War Two. The factory is most impressive and immense with its fathomless door vault in which nearly six million doors circulate. Andrew Stanton noted with regard to the film that 'I think somewhere midway through *Monsters*, we all started to sense, if we didn't watch ourselves, you'll be able to peg a Pixar movie'. This is an interesting note as it hints at Pixar's authorial identity where, typically, authorship would be regarded largely in terms of repeating stylistic patterns, character types, themes and tones.

In *Toy Story* and *Toy Story 2* human figures were present, albeit very much on the periphery in the original and, in the sequel, a little more centrally. In *Monsters, Inc* the young child, Boo, is central to the story although, wisely, is not rendered in a naturalistic way. Instead, she is obviously a cartoon, a caricature of a cute toddler.

Monsters, Inc begins with a delightfully inventive credit sequence that alludes to various key story elements in the movie in a style redolent of 1960s movies.

The action begins with a shot of toys positioned neatly on a shelf. We are looking in on a blissfully serene bedroom in which a little boy sleeps. We then see what appears to be a monster's arm slide out from the cupboard just beyond the foot of the boy's bed. The playfully odd feeling of the moment extends when we then discover that the little boy is in fact a robot that looks like a little boy. It turns out that the artificial kid scares the monster more than the monster scares him! What we are being shown is a training session for newly inducted monsters at Monsters, Inc to prepare them in how to scare children. Waternoose, the owner of Monsters, Inc, interrupts the session and establishes a key plot point: always close the cupboard door or else a child could get into Monstropolis and contaminate it.

This prologue then introduces us to the film's hero and sidekick, Sulley and Mike. Sulley is asleep and Mike is trying to wake him for another day at work. Their relationship is amusingly established and the film's deft interweaving of character and plot lays itself out with a shot of Mike and Sulley walking along that also includes a foreground element momentarily showing a newspaper headline that reads 'Scream shortage looms'. It transpires that Monstropolis, the city in which the monsters live, is fuelled by the screams of children from around the world. Monstropolis is running low on energy, though, and needs to replenish its resources. Sulley is Monsters, Inc's top scarer, followed closely by sneaky, creepy Randall Boggs, a chameleon-like monster who is jealous of Sulley's success. Indeed, jealousy features as a motivator for several villains in Pixar movies.

At the factory, Sulley reports for his shift and we see the scaring process in action. We then also see the monsters quickly turning scared when a child's sock is unwittingly brought onto the scare floor. We are reminded of Waternoose's stern reminder in the film's prologue.

Sulley's easygoing life abruptly shifts. He momentarily returns to the scare floor after finishing his shift and sees Randall Boggs fixing his score of scares. Productivity is key. In a moment that builds on the recent sock incident, Sulley then unwittingly lets into Monstropolis a little girl from the human world. She proves hard to catch and return home. There can be no greater source of toxicity than a child and Boggs recognises this as his chance to see Sulley demoted and his career... well, sullied.

Sulley goes to tell Mike about the rogue child, in doing so interrupting and ruining a hot date that Mike is on. The word about the child, named Boo, is out. Realising the scale of chaos that they now need to clear up, Sulley and Mike take Boo back to Sulley's apartment and try not to scare her even though they are terrified of her. Sulley realises that Boo is not to be feared.

For Boo's protection, Sulley and Mike disguise her as a monster and take her to work the next day where she escapes and runs amok. Mike wants to send Boo back through any door he can so as to get things back to normal but Sulley insists she return to her own bedroom. Boo then goes missing at the factory. Her wanderings lead her to discover a secret tunnel that leads to the Scream Extractor, the device that Randall Boggs wants to use to collect all the screams simply by extracting them, without the need to send a monster to scare a child. Racing against time, Sulley tries to explain to Waternoose what is going on. Amidst the high energy of the situation there's a fleeting and powerful moment when Sulley has the chance to see how a child looks when he goes out and scares them. The expression on Sulley's face marks the monster's newfound awareness. Waternoose takes Boo to send her home and he exiles Sulley and Mike to the Himalayas, a suitably silly turn of events that's rather the equivalent of the talking dogs in Docter's other Pixar film, *Up*.

Mike and Sulley manage to return to Monsters, Inc only to find that Boo has in fact been put in front of the Scream Extractor. Sulley rescues her but Randall attacks him. Sulley and Mike then race to return Boo safely home, taking her up into the immense door-archive to find her door. A dazzlingly orchestrated action sequence ensues. Sulley is eventually evicted and order is restored. Sulley then confronts Waternoose who, it becomes clear, will do anything to keep the company going and generate profit. He does not mind scaring children.

With order finally restored, a new version of Monstropolis begins: the city is now powered by laughter and not by screams.

Sulley is very much the child in this film and his buddy Mike is far more the older, slightly more wised-up 'brother'. He is a bear-like, warm character, which amplifies the mean spiritedness shown towards him later in the film.

One of the pleasures of Pixar films is the way in which they tap into the sensibilities of other films. The climactic chase sequence in *Monsters, Inc*, through the archive of closet doors, is a suspenseful, kinetic and visually dynamic achievement as well realised and shaped as the fast and furious mine car chase in *Indiana Jones and the Temple of Doom* (Steven Spielberg, 1984). Certainly, it recalls the whoosh and thunderous roar of a rollercoaster ride clattering frantically at a theme park, but the jeopardy is rooted in more than just a fleeting visual thrill. Sulley must rescue Boo so as to make good on his latent paternalism.

Like the *Toy Story* saga, *Monsters, Inc* deals with ideas and realities common to all children, in this case the experience of being scared and knowing fear. Sulley also learns the value of being responsible for someone and of doing more than scaring, a realisation that comes to him in the film's most affecting moment when he watches video playback of himself really being frightening. As with *Toy Story*, the power of the imagination is central to the resonance of *Monsters, Inc*. The film emphasises the playfulness of the monsters and it's worth acknowledging the connection that this playful film has with deeper-rooted traditions of narrative. Marina Warner writes about how, for children, 'testing the limits of safety and entertaining the terror of murder and torment help to confirm the child's sense of security with the parent or caregiver'[106].

Throughout *Monsters, Inc* there are many non-verbal indicators of character and it's these elements that partly account for the film's cinematic storytelling. When Sulley, in a hurry, rushes into the restaurant to tell Mike about Boo, look at how Sulley's foot taps impatiently beneath the table. Also notice how, when he's in the Abominable Snowman's ice cave, Sulley's expressions run from rueful to guilty to sad with real human subtlety.

Randy Newman's playful, jazzy score lends the movie a retro-sensibility that connects it to the workplace movie comedies of the

1960s. By contrast, for the all-action set piece that concludes the movie, the score is charged with straight-faced intensity. Newman also provides the film, as he did for *Toy Story*, with a nifty theme song, entitled 'If I Have You'. Newman has composed numerous very American-flavoured scores for films such as *The Natural* (Barry Levinson, 1984) and *Avalon* (Barry Levinson, 1990) .

Released in autumn 2001 to very positive reviews, *Monsters, Inc* reaffirmed the deft narrative punch of the Pixar approach, finding a potent way for the fantasy setting to brim with very real emotion. As with mainstream reviews of *Toy Story*, *Toy Story 2* and *A Bug's Life*, *Monsters, Inc* was described as nothing less than another example of Pixar's move to the summit of American feature-film animation. The cultural historian Norman Klein, in his book *7 Minutes*, alerts us to the fact that 'cartoons are, above all, a narrative built around the expressive possibilities of the anarchic'.[107]

The critical response to *Monsters, Inc* recognised its combination of spectacle and human interest. In the *Guardian*, the film was described as being 'staggeringly generous with its witty lines, allusions, above all with its sheer visual spectacle'[108] In *Sight and Sound* it was described as 'an animated feature that fuses self-consciousness and cultural irony'[109] and Roger Ebert wrote of the film that it was 'cheerful, high energy fun'[110].

Monsters, Inc charts the journey of a character (Sulley) coming to understand something of the complexities and inconsistencies of the world, all within a fast-paced, elegantly structured narrative that revels in the mischievousness animation offers. Like Woody in *Toy Story*, he is someone whose innocence and good spirits are tested.

For all of the film's visual splash, panache and expansive scale, its most arresting image is that of Boo's bedroom, dominated by a wash of blue moonlight and punctuated by a delicate point of light emanating from a moon-shaped night-light by her bed. If there is one picture-book image in the film it is this, a visual ode to the sanctity of a child's room, a retreat from the world that might just, as in Jim Henson's film *Labyrinth*, also be a way to a wider world. If the fantastical comes knocking, it's worth heeding the call.

Finding Nemo (2003)

Directed by: Andrew Stanton, Co-Director: Lee Unkrich
Written by: Andrew Stanton, Bob Peterson and David Reynolds (screenplay); Andrew Stanton (story)
Produced by: Graham Walter, Associate Producer: Jinko Gotoh
Music by: Thomas Newman
Edited by: David Ian Salter
Production Design: Ralph Eggleston
Art Direction: Randy Berrett, Anthony B Christov and Robin Cooper
Cast: Albert Brooks (Marlin), Ellen DeGeneres (Dory), Alexander Gould (Nemo), Willem Defoe (Gill)

By the time of *Finding Nemo*'s move into development and production, Pixar had established an identifiable aesthetic sensibility that had proved commercially and critically popular around the world. As with its previous titles, *Finding Nemo*'s particular appeal was evident at first glance, and perhaps more so than ever given the story's focus on a father and son. The film was notable for being the feature-film directing debut of Andrew Stanton who had co-directed and written earlier Pixar successes (*Toy Story*, *A Bug's Life*) and who would go on to write and direct *Wall-E* (2008) and the hugely entertaining fantasy adventure *John Carter* (2012). (Oh, how the studio should have retained the remaining words '*of Mars*' in its title. It's a film destined for the right kind of recognition in the years to come.)

A reverie of the marine world (akin to *The Little Mermaid*, which had been hugely popular in late 1989), the story of *Finding Nemo* centres on a quest and a rescue mission – a premise that has also been deployed well in three other Pixar films: *The Incredibles*, *Up* and *Toy Story 2*. Whilst it was never something harped upon at the time of the film's original release, there is something particularly American in this narrative of rescue from captivity, being a story structure that reaches right back to captivity narratives of the eighteenth and nineteenth centuries, dramatising the contact between white settlers and first nations. Movies like *The Searchers* (John Ford, 1956) and the very much more recent *Cowboys and Aliens* (Jon Favreau, 2011) both offer other well-known examples of this kind.

Certainly there's a rich psychological seam being mined by *Finding Nemo* in its handling of the way in which fathers and sons relate, and it's within the context of this archetypal relationship that the fantasy of the scenario becomes meaningful to the viewer. Given the generation of filmmakers working at Pixar, one of the fascinations of the studio's work is the way in which its films evidence the influence on their producers (and writers and directors) of the films directed, written and produced by George Lucas and Steven Spielberg during the 1970s and 1980s. A quest to rescue lost children features strongly in a number of Steven Spielberg films: *Poltergeist* (Tobe Hooper, 1982), *Hook* (1991) and *War Horse* (2012). And the space adventures of Lucas's *Star Wars* films resound.

As with other Pixar films, *Finding Nemo* augments vivid, classically styled animation technique, rendered using computer graphics, with a story anchored in the expression of long-held truths. Conceived by Andrew Stanton prior to the release of *Toy Story*, the film's focus on the adventures of a child determined to find his way back home recalls Don Bluth's animated adventures *An American Tail* (1986) and *The Land Before Time* (1988) and also Disney's *Pinocchio* (Ben Sharpsteen, 1940), which itself features its share of underwater action. Of this desire to return home, the psychologist Bruno Bettelheim has written of separation anxiety and of how 'the younger we are, the worse is our anxiety when we feel abandoned, for the young child actually dies when not sufficiently protected'.

In describing the film's genesis, Stanton couched it in terms of his experience of being a father. 'When my son was five, I remember taking him to the park. I had been working long hours and felt guilty about not spending enough time with him. As we were walking, I was experiencing all this pent-up emotion and thinking "I-miss-you, I-miss-you", but I spent the whole walk going "Don't touch that. Don't do that. You're gonna fall in there." And there was this third-party voice in my head saying "You're completely wasting the entire moment that you've got with your son right now." I became obsessed with this premise; that fear can deny a good father from being one. With that revelation, all the pieces fell into place and we ended up with our story.'[111] Critical to the emotional authenticity of the film is the believability of the father-son relationship and the sense of a little boy lost in a rather large world, an issue of scale evident from the film's earliest moments. The diminutive hero seeking a place to call home also characterises *Toy Story*, *Ratatouille* and *A Bug's Life*.

As a technical, and therefore an aesthetic, challenge the animators had to find inventive ways to make fish as fully expressive as possible, and certainly the anthropomorphing process plays its part. One has only to look at the typically extensive conceptual art produced during preproduction to identify critical moments that are dynamically realised in the eventual movie.

For example, check out Simon Varela's dense charcoal concept art for Nemo, including one showing a tiny Nemo in the foreground, trapped in a tuna net with massive tuna fish all around him, whilst, in the background, in the upper left of the image, is the fishing boat on stormy seas. We see above and below the surface in one drawing. The sense of scale in Varela's image is captured in the finished film. In terms of the film's attention to the physical and optical laws of nature, look at one of Ralph Eggleston's pastel drawings made during conceptual development on the film. The image is a beautiful rendition of the effects of light and shadow as a lattice of light plays on the surface of a whale.

A particularly satisfying aspect of *Finding Nemo*, then, is to be had in its representation of marine life and terrain, and the film consistently impresses in terms of creating a sense of density, distance and the play of sunlight. At the time of the film's theatrical release in May 2003, John Lasseter commented that, 'Our challenge was to let the audience know that our ocean is caricatured. We wanted them to know that this wonderful world doesn't exist, but then using the amazing tools that we have in computer animation make it look totally believable. Our goal is always to make things believable, not realistic. By stylising the design of things, adding more geometry and pushing the colours, we were able to create a natural and credible world for our characters.'[112]

Finding Nemo is a beautiful film. If you take the time to look at the developmental art work for a given Pixar film you'll see that they're often rendered in pastels. Certainly, *Finding Nemo* retains that illustration-focused, painterly style, even though the film has been made in the computer. As natural-world settings, the film's vividly rendered backgrounds have an equivalent appeal to the wilderness backgrounds in films such as *Princess Mononoke* (Hayao Miyazaki, 1997) and *Bambi*.

Inevitably, a film's development period allows the filmmakers to strive for the best balance and relationship between the parts of the story and its whole, and Ralph Eggleston, who served as the film's production designer, made the following point:

> One of our first priorities was to make the fish seem appealing. Fish are slimy, scaly things and we wanted the audience to love our characters. One way to make them more attractive was to make them luminous. We ultimately came up with three kinds of fish – gummy, velvety and metallic. The gummy variety, which includes Marlin and Nemo, has a density and warmth to it. We used backlighting and rim lights to add to their appeal and take the focus off their scaly surface quality. The velvety category, which includes Dory, has a soft texture to it. The metallic group was more of the typical scaly fish. We used this for the schools of fish.[113]

In terms of the degree of visual realism that typically characterises the lighting and shading of a Pixar movie, Dylan Brown, supervising animator of *Finding Nemo*, has commented that:

> Another big factor for us was timing. With characters like Buzz, Woody or Sulley, you have an earth-based gravity. But fish underwater can travel three feet in a flash. You blink and the thing is gone. We were wondering how they did that and studied their movements on video. By slowing things down, we could figure it out. Our timing got very crisp as we learned how to get our fish

Toy Story (1995)

Cars (2006)

Toy Story 2 (1999)

Wall-E (2008)

Up (2009)

The Incredibles (2004)

Monsters, Inc. (2001)

Cars 2 (2011)

Finding Nemo (2003)

Monsters University (2013)

A Bug's Life (1998)

Toy Story 3 (2010)

Ratatouille (2007)

Brave (2012)

Day and Night (2010)

Partly Cloudy (2009)

For the Birds (2000)

One Man Band (2005)

La Luna (2011)

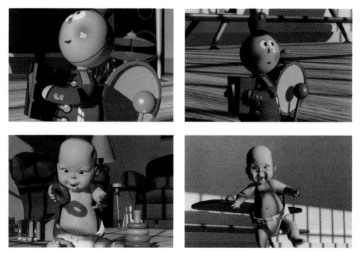

Tin Toy (1988)

Luxo Jr (1986)

Knick Knack (1989)

Gerri's Game (1997)

Presto (2008)

characters from one place to another in the course of a frame or two. We always tried to incorporate naturalistic fish movements into the acting. By putting things like one-frame darting and transitioning from one place to another into our acting, the characters became very believable.[114]

The film begins with an image of real lyricism as sunlight falls softly through the ocean depths. We then hear an adult male voice simply state, 'Wow.' As with Stanton's second Pixar film as director (*Wall-E*), sound is as critical as image to this very first moment of the film. We are then introduced to the source of the amazed voice: a clownfish named Marlin who is accompanied by his wife Coral. The couple are settling into a new coral-reef home and Coral describes it in such a way that it's as though they're moving into suburbia, referring to it as 'the new neighbourhood'. We then see a shot of a huge cluster of fish eggs; Marlin and Coral are waiting for them to grow. Marlin's essentially fretful temperament is established in this prologue when he says to Coral of the babies, 'What if they don't like me?' It's a laugh-line but it also captures a classic father-in-waiting anxiety. These fish are ultimately all too human in their doubts and fears, just like the toys, monsters and bugs in other Pixar films. Coral then sights a menacingly big fish moving threateningly close to her and Marlin, and she intuitively protects her babies. It's as though we're watching a natural history documentary, and it might be fair to say that we're very attuned to voiceovers humanising animals and the savage laws of nature... an illusion that might not be particularly useful for our understanding of actual animal life. Marlin gets sideswiped by the large fish and, when he comes to, finds Coral and the babies are gone. Marlin's discovery occurs at night, casting the sadness of the discovery in deep blue light to visually express the condition of his deep blue heart. Marlin cries and then sees that one egg has not been taken; it's a dot of red against the blue. Marlin immediately covers the egg with his fins and, in this moment, the film's sentimental grain is clear, with the story set to follow on from this image of protective father and fragile son.

The action then cuts, and young Nemo comes into frame as he embarks on his first day at school. Nemo is energetic and immediately his zesty movement embodies the energy of new life, of youth. Nemo's face and overall character design suggest yet another credible example of anthropomorphism at work in the Pixar aesthetic. His face is human-like in its expressivity and, as with all Pixar characters, much of this emotive work is carried by the actions of the eyes and the eyebrows.

The young school of fish head off and it's a moment that is somewhat redolent of the energy that begins the Disney studio adaptation of *Pinocchio* in which we watch the town awake. Nemo looks and sees a boat out in the distance beyond the reef and there is a real sense of it being a dangerous wilderness beyond the security of the reef. Against the wishes of his teacher, Nemo ventures out into the depths to investigate and swims right up to the boat's anchor chain, its links huge against Nemo. Nemo returns swiftly to the coral reef and, as he looks out one last time, the entire frame fills with the goggled face of a human ocean explorer and Nemo is taken. It's a monstrous, big-scare moment; a sort of kid-friendly equivalent of Ben Gardner's face appearing full frame in *Jaws* (Steven Spielberg, 1975). In its submarine sequences, *Finding Nemo* conjures that sense of potential menace just there beyond the haze and murky depths which *Jaws* trades on so powerfully.

Marlin sets out to find his son and encounters a fish named Dory who, to great comic effect, has a very short attention span. Where Marlin is driven and endlessly in motion, Dory dawdles and ponders as they try to recall information. Rather like Buzz and Woody in *Toy Story* they form a buddy partnership. Dory shows Marlin which way the boat went but we realise in this introductory moment how poor her memory is. Marlin and Dory encounter a group of sharks living in and around the hull of a sunken warship, an example of how the film enjoys differences in size.

The action then jumps to Nemo who finds himself 'imprisoned' in a fish tank in a dentist's office in Sydney, Australia. Unlike the opaque water of the ocean, the tank water is clear and this is our first clue as to his new whereabouts. Nemo is spooked by the fish-tank setting and scary sculptures and, soon afterwards, he meets his fellow neighbours. The fish are very anxious and Nemo is, very literally, a fish out of water, rather like Wall-E is aboard the *Axiom*.

The dentist who has caught Nemo shows him and the other fish a picture of his niece, Darla, and this apparently unassuming detail is a key story point that will be expanded later in the film. Finally, Nemo meets the 'big fish' of the tank and he's clearly a survivor, his nose marked by a massive scar.

The action then cuts back to Marlin and Dory, heading on with their quest to find Nemo. This is a rescue story, as are *Toy Story 2* and *The Incredibles*. Dory and Marlin learn that Nemo was last seen heading for Sydney and to get there must head for the East Australian Current. They do so and find themselves in the company of some very cool turtles in the film's 'heart scene', arguably the film's most resonant. Every Pixar film has such a scene, typically to be found at the midpoint of the film's running time, which becomes emblematic of the whole movie. This particular scene, in which the turtles encounter Marlin as they ride the East Australian Current deep in the ocean, is all about understanding the need to go with the flow in order to enjoy life's adventure: going with the flow doesn't mean a *laissez faire* attitude but rather an acceptance of change. As with *Aesop's Fables*, this animal-centred story expresses very human conditions, brimming with delight and echoing the 'big statement' moments of *Toy Story 2* ('Jessie's Song') and of *Ratatouille*.

The action then cuts to Nemo having his own perilous adventure within the fish tank as he goes to fix the jammed filter. At the last moment, however, the mission proves too dangerous.

Marlin and Dory finally arrive in Sydney and, in the dentist's office, Darla arrives to collect Nemo, the race-against-time dynamic suddenly building with increasing intensity. Nemo is bagged by Darla, who, we might say, is a more terrifying version of the menacing baby of the Pixar short *Tin Toy*, which was so critical to establishing the studio's creative identity.

Nemo ends up in the water of the harbour and Dory doesn't realise who he is whilst, of course, we, the audience, are desperate for her to recognise him. It's a classic moment of dramatic irony that turns the screws of tension, making us both fret and chuckle at the scenario.

The tension builds. Nemo gets caught in a fish net and Marlin struggles to free him. Amusingly, collective action by the fish helps liberate Nemo, who is momentarily lying exhausted on the sea bed in a moment of stillness that echoes Marlin's first moment with the Nemo egg at the beginning of the film.

Underpinning, and enhancing, the onscreen action is the music score composed by Thomas Newman. Across the body of his work, Newman's music has always been characterised by a compelling, quirky augmentation of more traditional melodies. His music is lyrical or urgent as required and, of his working process, Newman has described how, 'My approach normally is to start from a point of colour, meaning do I hear woodwind sounds or do I hear plucking sounds or bell sounds, and I try to build up. I normally start from a point of colour as opposed to a point of melody, and that's probably because I figure at some point I'll have to write melody anyway, so it's kind of a given, whereas colour is just fun to think about. What would happen if I did this or that, and what would happen if I used this kind of instrument?'[115]

Where Randy Newman's scores for the *Toy Story* films and *Monsters, Inc* had been jaunty and Americana-influenced, Thomas Newman's score for *Finding Nemo* emphasises the film's less frantic quality; there's something more tonal and hypnotic about his style; it has an ambient quality. Making use of percussion and unexpected chord progressions, Newman's score plays on the melancholy qualities of the story. *Finding Nemo*, like the films that preceded and followed it, was another immense commercial success for Pixar and reviews again acknowledged the film's visual fascination and resonant, all-too-human story.

It's certainly a long way from a Pixar movie, but it's an appropriate way to end the chapter. Here's the American novelist Herman Melville alerting us to the beauties and mysteries of the sea: 'Consider the subtleness of the sea; how its most dreaded creatures slide under water, unapparent for the most part and

treacherously hidden beneath the loveliest tints of azure.' There's
something in this nineteenth-century writer's feeling for the ocean
that finds an echo in *Finding Nemo*.

The Incredibles (2004)

Directed by: Brad Bird
Written by: Brad Bird
Produced by: John Walker
Music by: Michael Giacchino
Sound by: Randy Thom
Edited by: Stephen Schaffer
Production Design: Lou Romano
Art Direction: Ralph Eggleston
Cast: Craig T Nelson (Mr Incredible/Bob Parr), Holly Hunter (Elastigirl/
Helen Parr), Samuel L Jackson (Frozone/Lucius Best), Jason Lee
(Syndrome/Buddy Pine), Spencer Fox (Dash Parr), Sarah Vowell (Violet
Parr), Elizabeth Pena (Mirage), Brad Bird (Edna Mode)

This book has been written at a time when the Hollywood studios
are producing and releasing mega-successful superhero films with
understandable regularity. *Thor*, *Captain America*, *The Avengers* and
The Dark Knight have all been commercially profitable adaptations of
established American comic strips. Sitting just outside of this cluster
of films is a movie that predates them all: *The Incredibles* remains
one of the very best superhero films, being both pastiche and parody.

With *Toy Story*, *A Bug's Life*, *Toy Story 2*, *Monsters, Inc* and
Finding Nemo all confirmed as surefire successes, by the time of
the release of *The Incredibles* in autumn 2004 there was a sense,
perhaps, that Pixar had found a distinct creative and production-
process comfort zone in terms of the kinds of genres that best
suited their kind of animation and also the approach brought to
crafting the material. At the time of its release *The Incredibles* was
notable for being the first Pixar film to focus on human characters
and, around the time of the film's production, comments were
made that Brad Bird had partly been brought into the studio to reset

the Pixar production-process mindset, coming as he did from a cel-animation background. It might, more broadly, have been a different sensibility that Pixar was investing in. Wired magazine had this to say about Bird: 'Outspoken and high spirited, Bird calls himself "the first virus let into the climate-controlled atmosphere".'[116] Tellingly, The Incredibles remains perhaps the least sentimental of Pixar's films. Indeed, we might be about right to put it in company with Ratatouille and Cars 2 (2011) in this regard.

By the time production began on The Incredibles, Bird's own background in animation had already been well documented and celebrated, at least in animation-industry circles. Like John Lasseter, Glen Keane and Tim Burton, Bird had studied at Cal Arts in the 1970s. Indeed, in a significant way, this gathering of animators and directors recalls the conjunction of filmmakers at USC in Los Angeles in the mid-1960s. That constellation of talent included George Lucas, John Milius, Carroll Ballard and Walter Murch.

By the time he arrived at Pixar, Brad Bird had worked on two TV series, The Simpsons and Family Dog, and had co-written, with Matthew Robbins, the screenplay for batteries not included (which one might imagine as a Pixar film, and which started life as an Amazing Stories half-hour TV episode before being developed into a fully realised feature film; it might have been more rewarding remaining as a half-hour piece), as well as writing and directing the well-received but not especially popular The Iron Giant, which has since become something of a cult film. In relation to The Incredibles, it's worth reflecting on The Iron Giant a little more at this point in that it, too, is a movie about the nature of heroism and the complications inherent in being an outsider. This idea of the outsider underpins The Incredibles as well, with this character type taking the form of the superhero. The film relishes taking this icon of American popular culture and pastiching and parodying it. Of his time working on The Simpsons, Bird has narrated his experience as follows:

Jim Brooks and Sam Simon had seen Family Dog and liked its cinematic style. People don't remember, but at that particular time television animation had an incredibly rudimentary visual style; every story started with an establishing shot, medium shots when the characters travelled, close ups when they talked – the camera cutting to whoever's talking, etc, all done at eye-level. There were no long takes, no fast cutting... it was all dictated by what could be produced quickly and cheaply. *Family Dog* was just the opposite, it had extreme camera angles with pushed perspective, looooonnnnnggg uninterrupted shots, rapid-fire cutting at certain points, massive pans... everything under the sun. I was a huge fan of Jim Brooks and also of Matt Groening's comic strip *Life in Hell*. So when they asked me if I'd be interested in helping out on *The Simpsons* I jumped at the chance. I was not as familiar with Sam Simon's work, but I very quickly realised that he was a brilliant guy as well, and an unsung hero in those crucial early seasons of the show. *The Simpsons* one-minutes for Tracey Ullman were really funny, but turning them into a full-fledged series was a big challenge – a half-hour show is exponentially more complicated than a one-minute film. The scripts were brilliant. What I think I brought to it was a cinematic style that helped tell these very sophisticated stories in a uniquely visual way. The show already had two very talented directors in David Silverman and Wes Archer, who had worked on the one-minutes, but I think I was a valuable sounding board for supervising the visual storytelling. I looked at the episodes as miniature movies and I pushed the storyboard artists into looking at filmmakers like Kubrick and Welles for inspiration, rather than emphasising that they had to get it out fast. We all had to work our collective asses off to get the show out, but I recognised that the material and vocal performances were way better than anything I'd ever gotten to do at Disney, and knew it was a golden opportunity.[117]

Throughout the 1990s Bird had developed a number of animated projects, none of which had been realised, notably a film concept entitled *Ray Gunn*, a science-fiction film noir fusion that focused on a gun with an intelligence of its own. As such, maybe the omnidroid of *The Incredibles* ever so slightly follows through on that idea of technology with a brain.

If the robot is a hugely iconic figure that emerged in the twentieth century, then it's just about been superseded by the iconic image of the American comic-book superhero. Various and numerous film and television adaptations of comic-book and comic-strip source material have been produced over the decades, notably the Fleischer Studios animated adaptations of *Popeye* (1933) and *Superman* (1940s), Richard Donner's live-action *Superman: The Movie* (1978), Tim Burton's *Batman* (1989) and Sam Raimi's *Spiderman* saga (2002–07). Raimi's movies marked a moment when studio funding for comic-book adaptations took on new weight, and we might say that, across the board, comic-book adaptations have maybe reached their apogee with the gargantuan popularity of *The Avengers* (Joss Whedon, 2012). Whereas that film played it straight, *The Incredibles* serves to spike the genre; to deflate its self-importance a little bit.

Interestingly, *The Incredibles* was released just at that moment when live-action comic-book adaptations were beginning to prove very commercially viable, as evidenced by *Spiderman* and *Spiderman 2*. However, their success would duly be eclipsed by the commercial popularity of films adapting Marvel comics titles in the yeas 2008–12.

In their design work for the film it's clear, from the material available, that Pixar were keen to honour familiar elements from the comics whilst, understandably, presenting them afresh. The character designs for *The Incredibles* were notable for their attenuated forms, and the world in which the action unfolded evoked a late 1950s/early 1960s design sensibility that allowed the film to evoke a more widely recognised spy/tech thriller feeling that would be familiar to audiences from James Bond movies and numerous TV series. In looking through Lou Romano's conceptual designs for the film there's a real sense of the concept crystallising of a movie that would hark back to the genre cinema of this era. There's another dynamic Romano conceptual gouache artwork which shows Mr Incredible up against Ominidroid, the image really capturing scale, movement, mood, jeopardy, foreground and background. It could almost be a frame grab from the eventual film.

Scott Caple's sketch of Edna Mode's house suggests Frank Lloyd Wright's Fallingwater and also the house that features in *North by Northwest* (Alfred Hitchcock, 1957). In terms of the character designs for the film, the maquettes ably captured character in stasis: one can see the proof of this in Ken Melton's maquette of Violet, which describes her withdrawn nature, her arms tightly crossed, her posture slightly stooped, her glance furtive.

Like *Finding Nemo* and *Up* (which deals with the subject more metaphorically), *The Incredibles* centres around a father-son relationship and the notion of family, biological or otherwise. Where *The Incredibles* is perhaps a little more 'challenging' is that it dares to suggest that excellence is not a condition everyone experiences; it's a good example of how animation can articulate ideas in a way that a live-action film might not. *The Incredibles* celebrates elitism and also gently satirises suburban life, an aspect of the film that recalls a recurring feature of *The Simpsons*. In the book *Prime Time Animation*, Michael Tueth writes of *The Simpsons* that 'animation increased the opportunity for much more physical comedy, rapid dialogue, and plot twists than live action comedy could ever manage. It also offered a new view of family life.'[118] Indeed, the film comically dramatises the dynamics of familial relations. Brad Bird commented at the time of the film's theatrical release that 'the part that I'm interested in is all the personal stuff. I tried to base the powers on family archetypes.'[119]

The Incredibles begins and we hear Michael Giacchino's score before we see an image, and this very first moment of the film suggests mystery. A newsreel sequence (Bird uses a similar device to establish key story points for *Ratatouille* and the device is also used in *Up*) shows Mr Incredible being interviewed and complaining that 'every superhero has a secret identity. Who wants the pressure of being super all the time?' There is then a newsreel interview with Mrs Incredible and then with their superhero buddy, Frozone. Adding to the charm of these interviews are the asides each character makes. Paradoxically, something as designed and planned as animation is being used to suggest a sense of serendipity and spontaneity. Mrs Incredible makes a pertinent point that will carry through the film, asking rhetorically, 'Leave saving the world to the men? I don't think so.'

The film's logo and title then fill the screen and there is a cut to a thrillingly fast-paced car-chase shoot out. The action takes us inside Mr Incredible's car as he prepares for crime-fighting action. As the tension ratchets up, Mr Incredible, in a parody of Superman, breaks from his hardheaded pursuit of the criminals to go and rescue a cat from a tree. It's this collision of high-octane action with the humour of the mundane that deflates the superheroics and characterises the film as a brilliantly realised action comedy. Returning to fighting crime, Mr Incredible finds that Incrediboy (Buddy from the Incredibles fan club) is sitting in the passenger seat of his car. Mr Incredible promptly ejects Incrediboy from the car, dismissing his interest in, and enthusiasm for, the Incredibles and superheroes in general. It's a powerful little comment on the perils of meeting your heroes and it gives Buddy the psychological motivation for what he goes on to do.

The action then cuts from Mr Incredible's exploits and we are introduced to Elastigirl who we see take out a thief. In the next moment, she and Mr Incredible are bickering on a sunset-lit rooftop in a conversation enhanced and warmly parodied by a musical underscore that evokes the spirit of John Barry's musical compositions for the James Bond films. We think that Elastigirl and Mr Incredible are chatting each other up but it emerges that they are already a couple. Frozone then passes through and Mr Incredible's exploits for the evening continue as he goes and saves a suicide. This event is seemingly 'incidental' but, in this film, the storytelling structure is particularly confident, with every detail contributing to the whole, and the suicide scene is a fantastic piece of foreshadowing and not exactly the kind of story content you'd expect in a film for young people... but is it only for young people? Mr Incredible works in the generic city of Municiberg and, whilst the era in which the story is set is not specified or made explicit, there's a feeling that it's notionally the 1960s. Indeed, James

Bond first appeared onscreen in the film *Dr No* in 1962, and so the association conjured makes sense. Mr Incredible's final mission for the evening involves confronting the bank robber Bomb Voyage, the first of the film's playful superhero/supervillain names. Incrediboy then turns up again, saying to Mr Incredible, 'I am your ward.' It's a comment that riffs on the Batman and Robin relationship so familiar to many of us from comics, films and television, and it's another example of the film's self-aware knowingness, which enhances, rather than disrupts, the story world that has been created by Bird and his team.

Watch the film closely and notice how much expressive material is communicated through characters' hand gestures and eyebrow movements. These details are powerful and nicely combine both extremes of the spectrum characterising animation that Maureen Furniss has usefully noted in her book, *Art in Motion*, which defines animation as existing on a span that reaches from mimesis through to abstraction.[120]

Mr Incredible later turns up at church to marry Elastigirl. They bicker at the altar and Elastigirl advises him, 'If we're going to make this work you've got to be more than Mr Incredible', the exchange finding humour in the tension between work and home. Mr Incredible can't escape family duties by hiding behind his work.

We then watch more newsreel footage used as a device to provide subplot detail, in this case regarding Mr Incredible being sued by the failed suicide we saw him save earlier in the film. In turn, this leads to trouble for superheroes everywhere, and so the government hides them because of the threat of legal action. The superheroes are compelled to take on 'anonymous' real lives. This 'grounding' of the superheroic, of placing them squarely in the context of the ordinary, connects to graphic novel *The Watchmen* (1986) and also the novel *American Gods* (2001) by Neil Gaiman. Perhaps less well known is the New Universe series of comic titles published by Marvel Comics in 1986, which sought to make superheroics feel more 'ordinary': titles included *Merc, Spitfire and the Troubleshooters* and *Justice*, to name just several in the series.

The action of the film then jumps to 15 years later and we reunite with Bob Parr who is now working as an insurance agent. His hair has thinned and his hands express his frustration, more so than what he says ever does. Watch how they clench and flex as he listens to an old lady complain about how the insurance company treats her. The vibrant colours of the world in which he was Mr Incredible have been replaced by drab, grey, monochrome surroundings and Bob's bully of a little boss is a grey bureaucrat who criticises him for being too eager to help (i.e. be heroic).

The action then cuts to Mrs Parr at school in a meeting with the headteacher about Dash being problematic. It's the moment of realisation that Dash can run incredibly quickly, and it's a scene that illustrates well the storytelling principle of show don't tell: we could easily have heard about Dash's ability, but instead we see it in action. As Dash walks away from the meeting, he comes right into the foreground and smiles. In the family car, Dash looks out of the passenger window and talks with his mum about not doing sports because he will win every time. Dash is experiencing the 'classic' Superman dilemma: what do you do with a gift if it means you'll stand out so much from everyone else? Dash's mum tries to rationalise the situation for him by saying, in a matter-of-fact way, 'Everyone's special, Dash.' To which Dash, all too cleverly, replies, 'Which is another way of saying "No one is".' His rueful facial expression is foregrounded in the shot.

Contrasting with the high energy of Dash is his rather cautiously moving teenage sister, Violet, whose name readily conjures an association with the term 'shrinking violet' for someone who is shy. Violet has a crush on a boy at school (who dresses much like the Beat-dude in *The Iron Giant*) but does nothing about it; she feels disempowered despite her great gift. Where Dash wants everyone to know what he can do, Violet wants to keep it a secret. The film sees its characters come to celebrate their uniqueness and their being outside the mainstream.

There is then a cut to suburbia and a very amusing piece of visual humour ensues. Bob pulls up from his day at work. A toddler sitting on a little tricycle watches Bob become frustrated and finally lift the family car up and throw it in exasperation. The timing of the moment is exquisite, the little boy saying nothing, yet with his shock and surprise registered in his facial expression. Performance in animation.

That evening at the family dinner table Bob encourages Dash to be fast. Bob then leaves the table and reads a newspaper article about a superhero advocate who has gone missing. Lucius (Frozone) shows up and the two friends tell Mrs Incredible they're going bowling. What they actually do is go and listen to the police radio and intercede in a crime. They can't move on, or accept change. It's a film about getting older. However, they're being watched by a spy. Bob gets back home after a misadventure of sorts with Frozone to find Mrs Incredible waiting for him. He explains what he's been doing and she tells him he's missing out on his family. We then cut back to Bob in his insurance job where his boss comes to confront him again.

We then see Bob in his office at home, something of a dimly lit shrine to his youthful glories as a recognised superhero. This man clearly has a problem letting go. However, if we were feeling more charitable, we'd say that the scene is consistent with a storytelling hallmark of Pixar films, which is to create scenes and narrative arcs that see a character strengthened by an act of memory: Remy experiences this in *Ratatouille*, Mater in *Cars 2* and, most movingly perhaps, Carl in *Up*. Then, too, memory characterises 'Jessie's Song' in *Toy Story 2*. In Pixar movies, memory gives strength to characters and renews them for the adventure ahead. It's a storytelling device that we might also recognise from a number of films directed and produced by Steven Spielberg.

Sitting in the quiet of his office, as far from his adventurous past as he could possibly imagine, Bob finds a package on his desk and looks inside it. What he finds, appropriately, given Steve Jobs' investment in Pixar, is what looks rather like an iPad and it sparks to life. It's a communication device and it carries a message for Bob from a mysterious woman called Mirage. She talks about Bob's unique abilities and then about the threat of the Omnidroid, which needs to be immobilised (it's just a bait to get him to Syndrome's island). The camera pushes in on Bob, emphasising the import of the moment. The camera then elegantly circles him to reveal his wall of pictures as a heroic musical motif plays on the soundtrack. It's a breakthrough moment for Bob who proceeds to tell his wife that he's being sent to a conference (a lie... a bit like *True Lies* [1994]). She hugs him and is filled with pride that his career is progressing. However, what's emphasised in the shot is Bob's guilty look.

From the calm of suburbia the action then cuts to Bob on a plane with Mirage – and he's got his outfit back on from the old days. Now back in his Mr Incredible identity, Bob is deployed to the jungle looking for Omnidroid. As he confronts the robot, however, we realise it's a trap set by Syndrome.

Helen is then summoned by an old contact named Edna Mode who explains Bob's predicament and gives Helen a new suit. In effect, Edna fulfils a mythic function as the bestower of wisdom and of a gift to help Helen with the adventure ahead. The action then amplifies the ever-raising stakes by taking us back to the island where Bob discovers that all of the superheroes who were his contemporaries have been terminated by Omnidroid. The filmmaker's pleasure in giving names that sound suitably superheroic and also amusing is evident. The action then cuts back to Helen. Having learned where Bob is, she duly sets out to rescue him.

Helen travels to the island only to find that her kids have stowed away to join her. As Helen embarks on her rescue mission she quickly recognises that her family is 'the adventure', rather as Ellie shows in her Adventure Book in *Up*.

As Helen, Violet and Dash set about rescuing Bob, there's a sequence, presented with great dynamism, in which Dash is chased through the jungle. Dash runs on water, delighting in abilities that might remind you of Superman running faster than a locomotive in *Superman: The Movie*. It's not so much a case of 'Look, Ma, no hands!' as 'Look, Ma, no terra firma!' as he races so quickly he's almost flying. The scene is propelled by the music, of which its composer Michael Giacchino, sketching out his involvement with the film, said:

> When I first met with Brad, he asked me what I grew up listening to. I told him I loved the *Pink Panther* movies, *Star Wars*, *Jonny Quest*, *The Flintstones*, *The Jetsons*, *The Twilight Zone* – all these things. And we quickly realised that he and I both had a love for those 1960s jazz orchestra scores. It was an amazing time, when they were just going for it, with those jazz influences. No one was saying, "Oh, that sounds cheesy" – it was what it was, and you believed in it, and just went with it. Brad's point was, when he was a kid he would hear that theme to *Jonny Quest* and would want to be Jonny Quest. And that's what he wanted for *The Incredibles*. He wanted the orchestral jazz energy that they used to have in the Bond movies, *Pink Panther* movies, and everything else I mentioned – the quasi-big band stuff. That's what he wanted in the score to his film.[121]

As this mid-movie action focus unfolds it becomes evident that Syndrome misunderstands the idea of what it is to be heroic and super.

The action then cuts back to the city where Omnidroid is causing chaos and destruction in a sequence somewhat informed by 1950s science-fiction and horror films. The film builds towards a near-apocalyptic conclusion.

Omnidroid is duly destroyed but the stakes are raised one more time when Bob and Helen realise that their son Jack-Jack's in trouble: Syndrome has invaded the sacred family home where Jack-Jack is.

In the film's epilogue we see Jack at a sporting event and another bad guy turns up – time for another adventure.

In an online piece about the film, Tom Elrod commented that, '*The Incredibles* is probably Pixar's most difficult film to pin down politically, but it is not John Lasseter and co's only film to be read as conservative.'[122] Elrod goes on to note that both *Ratatouille* and *The Incredibles* are about being extraordinary as opposed to just ordinary.

The Incredibles celebrates being different and suggests that revelling in one's difference and individuality is to be cherished. What fascinates about *The Incredibles* is that it is a film distributed by Disney, and clearly branded as one of their releases, though not produced by them. Yet in Disney animated films there is a kind of equality expressed between the characters. In *The Incredibles*, on the other hand, it is expressed quite overtly that some are more gifted than others.

According to Roger Ebert, 'On the surface, *The Incredibles* is good on superhero comics. Underneath, it's a critique of modern American uniformity.'[123] In the *Guardian* the film was described thus: 'All I can say is: for those of you looking for the classic holiday movie, call off the search...'[124] And in the *New York Times* the reviewer commented: 'Anything but dull and ordinary, this computer animated feature... is organised around a strong, fascinating idea.'[125]

The Incredibles is a film with human characters at its centre, not inanimates or anthropomorphised creatures, and is perhaps more obviously made with an adult audience in mind. It marked the beginning of the real fêting of Pixar, the studio having proved beyond doubt that it had staying power beyond *Toy Story*. And from here on, also, there was a tangible sense that people were now waiting for Pixar to 'fail'.

Cars (2006)

Directed by: John Lasseter and co-directed by Joe Ranft
Written by: Dan Fogelman, John Lasseter, Joe Ranft, Kiel Murray, Phil Lorin, Jorgen Klubien
Produced by: Darla K Anderson
Music by: Randy Newman
Sound by: Tom Myers
Edited by: Ken Schretzmann
Production Design: William Cone and Bob Pauley
Cast: Owen Wilson (Lightning McQueen), Paul Newman (Doc Hudson), Bonnie Hunt (Sally Carrera), Larry the Cable Guy (Mater), Cheech Marin (Ramone), Tony Shalhoub (Luigi), George Carlin (Fillmore)

Given the capacity of movies to incorporate, invoke and connect with an expansive range of cultural reference points, Pixar films consistently find spaces for this opportunity. Automobiles and American culture enjoy an elaborate and somewhat mythic relationship. As a nation whose muscular economy and global reach was so definitive of the twentieth century, being able to travel great distances had been key and the car became an icon. Henry Ford, the legendary American industrialist and manufacturer of cars, once said of the automobile that 'the Model T… had stamina and power. It broke down the barriers of distance in rural sections, brought people of these sections closer together and placed education within reach of everyone.' This gets a little at the allure which the vehicle holds, and which is central to the appeal of John Lasseter's *Cars*.

In the *Toy Story* trilogy we can readily see the influence of American illustrator Norman Rockwell's work and, in *Cars*, the Rockwell influence and sensibility is again vividly evident. Of Rockwell's important, enduring connection to American popular culture the art critic Robert Hughes noted in his book *American Visions: The Epic History of Art in America* that 'Rockwell was a national name and by the end of the Depression was an institution. In the 1950s he shared with Walt Disney the astonishing distinction of being one of the two visual artists familiar to nearly everyone in the United States.' Another frame of reference for us, in terms of the film's anthropomorphised vehicles, is the influence of John Tenniel and Jean Ignace Isidore Gerard on the idea of the anthropomorphised animal.[126]

Cars, then, builds on a well-established animated film tradition of using automobiles as humanised characters, and they do indeed lend themselves well to being anthropomorphised. Other titles include Tex Avery's *One Cab's Family* (1952), *Streamlined Greta Green* (Friz Freleng,1937) and *Suzie the Little Blue Coupe* (1952).

If the eyes are really the window of the soul then there's plenty of evidence demonstrating how particularly vivid and expressive the eyes of Pixar's characters are. From Nemo's innocent eyes to Buzz Lightyear's self-important raised eyebrow and Remy the rat's slightly nervy look, each Pixar hero and heroine has much of their identity defined simply by their eyes. Similarly, in *Cars*, each character has an eyebrow effect that assists in defining their emotion and thought.

In developing *Cars*, John Lasseter was prompted to see the confluence of filmmaking and personal life having taken a road trip with his family after the immensely busy period that covered the production of *Toy Story*, *A Bug's Life* and *Toy Story 2*. This kind of observation seems to indicate the idea of authorship not only in terms of autobiography but also aesthetic choice.

The film is as much about identity as *Toy Story*, *Ratatouille* and *The Incredibles* are.

The film's visual style rests on a photorealistic lighting and shading aesthetic that we're familiar with from across Pixar's body of work and also an alluring imagining of rural America. *Cars* revels in the romanticisation of American small-town life and the romance of a beautifully designed car and the roar of its engines. Kristin Thompson wrote of the film: 'The vehicles parade up and down the main street, and the reflections run over their surfaces from every side. (This segment and the design of the town's drive-in restaurant irresistibly recall the appealing look of *American Graffiti*.)'[127]

The film begins with a series of fast-paced, intercut shots, which move back and forth between the details of a gleaming chassis and wide shots showing a NASCAR-styled race roaring past. It's a brash introduction and establishes the tone of the film but, more importantly, the world that its protagonist comes from. There is then a cut to darkness and we hear the voice of someone we will come to know as Lightning McQueen, the car-hero of the film. We are not entering into the cosy world of *Toy Story*'s bedroom setting or the pastoral idyll of Ant Island in *A Bug's Life*. There is then another cut to a briefly held shot of cars whipping around the track before the action cuts back to the darkness and we realise we are inside a lorry, its door opening for Lightning to emerge from.

We are at a race in the Piston Cup competition. The race is shown with great energy and Lightning McQueen wins to great adulation, and we swiftly get the sense that he thinks he is a bit better than the rest of the competition. A necessary mindset of the track but, off it, Lightning has a little of Bob Parr about him in that, like Bob (Mr Incredible), he's perhaps a bit too ready to relish his strengths instead of recognising his weaknesses.

We then see Lightning en route to his next race, crossing classic American landscapes. This sequence is given its particular flavour, not by an orchestral score (as we might expect and be familiar with from Lasseter's earlier films, *Toy Story*, *A Bug's Life* and *Toy Story 2*), but instead through the inclusion of rock songs that readily create a sense of time and place and tone. There's a contemporary quality being conjured here and this is necessary in order to emphasise the contrast that will soon become focal to the story. The rock song that is pivotal to this sequence is 'Life is a Highway', an effective and unsubtle indicator of what the film's subject is.

En route to the next race in California, Lightning accidentally rolls off his tour truck, named Mac, as they travel along Route 66 (the original title for the film). Lightning very soon finds himself unintentionally abandoned and far from Route 66. Albeit briefly, it's worth noting here some essential real-world Route 66 facts: the road begins in Grant Park, Chicago and stretches west to Santa Monica, covering a distance of 2,400 miles and covering eight of the United States. In the *Oxford Dictionary of American History* the road is described as follows: 'The physical character of Route 66 was probably always less important than its place in the imagination. Towns fought for the chance to become landmarks on this self-proclaimed "Main Street of America".'[128]

Having become separated from Mac, Lightning gets chased for speeding at the edge of Radiator Springs, and a simple but effective wide shot introduces us to the stillness and calm of the desert town as Lightning rather noisily and boisterously arrives in it. How at odds his reality is with that of the down-on-its-luck small town. He is swiftly impounded and soon after meets Mater, a goofy tow truck who has never heard of Lightning, much to the race car's chagrin. In this moment, though, a friendship that will come to stand as the equal of Buzz and Woody's is formed. These buddy connections celebrate the fact that, while we all live in different realities, we can still find ourselves striving for the common ground.

Lightning then finds himself in a courtroom where he is required to explain his reckless speed through the town. Presiding over the hearing is elderly Doc Hudson who is gruff and stern and who will emerge as the wisdom giver of the film, the source of solace and understanding for the younger characters. There's one such character in every Pixar film, as there are in many films. In the court, one good thing that does come to pass is that Lightning meets Sally and there is an immediate, underplayed attraction between them. Adding to the delicacy of the scene is the detail of light spilling around window frames and the attention paid to the WPA styled art on the walls of the garage.

Sally insists that Radiator Springs is 'a town worth fixing'. The brash world of the track has now been left behind and the film pits the urban against the pastoral.

Norman Klein has written that 'Domestic melodrama spoke very directly to the Depression era, which ended with the war, about nostalgia for an age presumably of greater simplicity, before the Crash, even before the automobile; an age that suggested prosperity (not true in fact, only in fantasy). It referred to rural values from the "good old days", to social conditions before the industrial expansion of the 1870s.'[129]

At the court hearing Lightning is sentenced to repair the road he ripped to pieces upon his arrival, and this marks the first stage of his being confronted with the need to 'get over' his ego. All he wants to do is get to California for the Piston Cup. Instead he is required to do nothing less than atone for his sin! Lightning is somewhat the prodigal son.

In the course of his efforts at fixing the road, Lightning injures himself. He then goes out by himself and races around the dirt track on the edge of town. Doc Hudson goes and talks to him. As the film develops we realise that driving functions as a pretty good metaphor for life: the need to adapt quickly to situations, to follow a pattern, to combine intellect with intuition, to make mistakes and correct them and, of course, to undertake a journey which will combine clear stretches where you cruise along with plenty of wrong turns, detours, potholes and problems.

Akin to Woody, Remy and Nemo, we might say that Lightning is very much a boyish character on his road to being a young man. What more of an expression of the studio's investment in the idea of American Romanticism could we wish to find? Lightning initially has no real regard for old man Hudson and so must discover why he should respect him. In doing so, Lightning is humiliated.

Apparently lacking in street smarts, Tow Mater is clever enough to note of Lightning that he is in love with Miss Sally.

Alone in the evening, Lightning and Sally exchange dialogue that captures the sense of nervous chit-chat between two people who recognise an attraction to each other. Counterpointing this sweetness, however, is a nightmare that Lightning has, which has a manic, momentary darkness to it that recalls the dips into darkness we've seen in the *Toy Story* movies.

As in each Pixar film – indeed, as in all stories that really work – there is a moment of epiphany and, in *Cars*, this occurs when Lightning McQueen comes across Doc's garage and a slow camera move pulls back to reveal the three Piston Cups of 1951, 1952 and 1953 which Doc won. Pixar's stories often hint at a nostalgia for the 1950s, which have become something of an idealised decade in American life.

Without resorting to dialogue, the image of the cups tells us that, in his time, Doc Hudson has been as good as, and perhaps better than, Lightning McQueen. This sense of past glories connects Doc's sadness to that of Bob Parr in *The Incredibles* and to the ghost of Gusteau in *Ratatouille*. Indeed, the dread of becoming redundant is also what fires much of Woody's fear in the *Toy Story* trilogy. In due course, Doc Hudson will recapture his glory days by reclaiming a moment in the spotlight. At this point in the story, though, Doc is probably clinically depressed and has completely detached himself from any sense of what his past means. 'All I see is a bunch of empty cups,' Doc says in a very melancholy way.

In contrast with Doc's sadness, the action then cuts to Sally and Lightning going out for a ride away from Radiator Springs and, significantly, the music accompanying this road trip is very different to the music that tracked Lightning's initial ride west. What we now hear on the soundtrack, composed by Randy Newman, is a piece of music that we could best describe as sounding distinctly 'American' somehow, but which, more specifically, we can say invokes the spirit of the work of composer Aaron Copland. (Copland's life in music spanned much of the twentieth century and his mid-century works for the concert hall and also for cinema contributed to what we might now call a classic Americana sound, rather in the way that Norman Rockwell's illustrations contributed to an iconic set of images of twentieth-century America. Copland's compositions include *Appalachian Spring*, *Rodeo*, *Billy the Kid* and *A Letter From Home*. Of his work in composing the music for Pixar movies, Newman has commented that 'orchestration is very important to me... I react entirely to what I see up there on the screen... Music is a philosophical medium.'

Lightning McQueen enjoys his road trip with Sally and is amazed at the expanse of the American landscape with its rock formations, waterfalls and trees. Indeed, the rock formations are golden. Sally points out that the Wheelwell Hotel is no longer in business and Lightning asks Sally, 'How does a Porsche wind up in a place like this?' Sally explains that she started out in LA but got tired of fast-lane life. She broke down (in every sense, we might assume) in Radiator Springs and never left. Lightning asks why she didn't go back to California and she explains that she 'fell in love with this'. As she explains her reasons for staying, there is a cut and the 'camera' pushes forward between them towards an immense vista of the beautiful American desert with the freeway cutting elegantly through it. Lightning regards the passing cars and says wistfully, 'They're driving right by – don't know what they're missing.' It's an adult kind of perspective rather than something that younger viewers will recognise. In this moment, the film boldly states its regret at the passing of a moment of time, and it's part of a larger

pop-culture narrative mourning the passing of the American small town that we also know from films such as *The Last Picture Show* (Peter Bogdanovich, 1971) and from songs like 'Ghost Towns on the Highway' and 'Small Town' by the singer-songwriter John Mellencamp. Sally explains to Lightning how Route 66 used to be and says that it was there 'not to make great time, but to have a good time'. Can it be that a film made in such a frenetic world is espousing the value of lingering a while, of stillness? The soundtrack of realistic sound then goes mute and the only sound we hear is an elegiac song sung by James Taylor. It has the same melancholy feeling and sense of loss as 'Jessie's Song' in *Toy Story 2*.

We next see an image of a new road being built, and then the image dissolves to show the empty road of Radiator Springs. The action then cuts to Doc Hudson racing around the dirt track. Lightning drives after him and then follows him back to his garage to ask him, or maybe confront him, about the trophies. Hudson is defensive: 'You think I quit?' he growls. On the wall is an old newspaper cutting containing the story of how Doc crashed and how, after the crash, he was never welcomed back to the world of racing. From that point on, he felt his life had been wasted. This sense of lost opportunity is also to be found in the character of Carl in *Up*. In that film, too, it drives everything he does and all of the ways in which he reacts to situations. Doc is an embittered old guy, that's for sure, and Lightning will eventually become something like the route back to a new life for Doc. We could even go as far as saying that theirs is akin to the relationship between Obi Wan and Luke in *Star Wars* (George Lucas, 1977).

Lightning, with a new perspective on the world, goes on to complete finishing the road and then is nowhere to be seen. Sally's expression tells us of her feelings about this, her brows slanted over her eyes as she drives off slowly (the pace at which the cars move across the screen typically being used to suggest their emotional state at any given moment). Lightning hasn't gone, however, having realised just what he has at Radiator Springs. He gets spruced up by his new friends and then, as his old buddy, Mac, arrives in town, there is the sense of a team gathering, of a family being reunited. Sally realises that Lightning must return to the world of the race track.

The press and media turn up at Radiator Springs and there's a shot of them crowding Lightning, followed by a wide shot looking down on the street and showing Sally there alone.

From this moment of quiet and stillness the film cuts to the high energy of the Piston Cup in LA, to which Lightning has travelled with his Radiator Springs buddies, including Doc Hudson, who is there as Lightning's coach.

During the race, Lightning comes to the aid of a crashed car rather than using his competitor's difficulties to his advantage. Dinoco signs him up – not because he won (which he didn't), but because he helped someone else. In the epilogue, we see Lightning back in Radiator Springs explaining to Sally that he'd like to stay. Her bashful look says all that we need to know.

Cars, then, embodies the American fascination with the automobile and reasserts the need to look back in order to then propel yourself forward.

The film was received more coolly than was typical for a Pixar film. Typical responses included this comment from the *Observer*: 'Drives along a knife-edge between satire and sentimentality...'[130] Roger Ebert commented: 'I wouldn't have thought that even in animation a 1951 Hudson Hornet could look simultaneously like itself and like Paul Newman but you will witness that feat.'[131] Meanwhile, in *Empire* magazine, the verdict was more overtly critical: 'Judged against previous form, this is not Pixar firing on all cylinders, lacking the sophisticated comedy we've come to expect.'[132]

Ratatouille (2007)

Directed by: Brad Bird
Co-directed by: Jan Pinkava
Written by: Brad Bird (screenplay); Jan Pinkava, Jim Capobianco, Brad Bird (story)

Produced by: Brad Lewis
Music by: Michael Giacchino
Edited by: Darren T Holmes
Production Design: Harley Jessup
Cast: Patton Oswalt (Remy), Ian Holm (Skinner), Lou Romano (Linguini), Brian Dennehy (Django), Pete Sohn (Emile), Peter O'Toole (Anton Ego), Brad Garrett (Gusteau), Janeane Garofalo (Colette), Will Arnett (Horst)

Animation history is replete with rodents. There's no question about that. Most famously there are Mickey Mouse and Minnie Mouse, first seen on the movie screen in 1928 and 1929 respectively, in *Plane Crazy*. Then, too, there's Mighty Mouse and Timothy Mouse, movie stars of the years 1942/3 and 1941 respectively. More recently, there's been Fievel Mouskewitz in *An American Tail* (Don Bluth, 1986), Mrs Frisby in *The Secret of NIMH* (Don Bluth, 1982), *Danger Mouse* (Cosgrove Hall, 1981) and *The Tale of Despereaux* (Sam Fell, 2008). Then, too, there's the country mouse and the town mouse as brilliantly animated by Ladislaw Starewicz (1926). Remy, the hero of *Ratatouille*, is a noble addition to the long list of rodent movie stars. What is it, then, about rodents that has such appeal? Don Bluth, director of *The Secret of NIMH* and *An American Tail*, offers a pretty fair assessment of the situation when he says, 'I think people like mice because they're the underdog… In an animated film all the animals are symbols for people.'[133] Where *Ratatouille* breaks with the movie history's tradition is in opting for a rat, as opposed to a mouse, as hero. The film is an affecting achievement and one of Pixar's best films yet. Certainly, it's the Pixar film that perhaps remains closest to the spirit of a fairy tale story.

It's the case that each Pixar film fits pretty neatly and inventively into a generic format, whether it be adventure, comedy or action movie. *Ratatouille* is a buddy movie and comedy that asks the question: 'What makes for friendship?'

When the film was released, mainstream press coverage actually took note of the director as author. Where does the balance lie between a particular work being a Pixar film and being the film of a named director? At the Disney studio, Walt Disney is 'assumed' to be the director of the films made during his lifetime, but this is not the case. Disney himself supervised production but you'll never see him credited as director on the animated feature films released between 1937 and 1966 (the year he died). However, this perception has been applied to animation globally for many years (Winsor McCay, Michel Ocelot, Caroline Leaf, etc) and it's certainly one of the fascinating things about Pixar: it's known as a studio but, within it, are various *auteur* directors, just as we might say there have been in the live-action world: Tim Burton with Warner Brothers, Steven Spielberg with Universal, James Cameron with Twentieth Century Fox.

Originally conceived and directed by Jan Pinkava, who had established his name with the Pixar short *Geri's Game*, *Ratatouille* was subsequently taken control of by Brad Bird who entirely rewrote the screenplay before commencing to 'redirect' the project. Working from the key story premise, Bird wrote a full new screenplay that sat alongside some already approved design work. In the original concept for the film, Gusteau was still alive but, in the process of revising the screenplay, Bird decided to have him be a ghost.

Of the film's eventual look, Harley Jessup, production designer on the film, commented that, 'As the colour script is being developed it goes through a very basic phase. From the beginning [...] I had wanted to explore a muted palette that reflected the subtle colours of Paris itself. Sharon Calahan, director of photography for lighting, suggested starting out with a simple concept that the rat world would be cool and the human world would be warm. This colour dynamic supported the idea that the rats are always on the outside looking in and made Remy's yearning to be part of the warm human world even more understandable.'[134]

The film began production in 2005. With the exception of two shots from previous work an entirely new story reel was produced, and very quickly. Of his contribution to the project Brad Bird has explained, 'I changed a lot about the way the story was structured. I kept a lot of stuff, but I changed a lot of things in order to get them to work. It had to do with emphasis... Part of the problem was many of the characters didn't have a defined personality.'

The film's story follows Remy the rat as he undertakes the journey from his country barnyard home to Paris, the city of light. This rural to urban quest is vintage folk tale material. Just think of Dick Whittington and Oliver Twist and you have two iconic examples. *Ratatouille* is, like *Cars* and *Finding Nemo*, about a character displaced from home; about where you're from and where you're going, and the relationship between looking to the future and remembering your roots. The film explores the importance of pursuing a dream and the idea of inspiration.

In an interview with National Public Radio (NPR) on 28 June 2007, right around the time of the film's theatrical release, Bird explained his casting of comedian Patton Oswalt as Remy: 'He was volatile about food and so passionate and funny about it, you know, it just struck me: "That's the character." He's so volatile, but in a good way. That kind of extreme emotion is perfect for Remy.' Oswalt's experience with stand-up comedy shines through in the confidence of the character.

In promotional material for the film, production manager Nicole Paradis-Grindle commented that, 'It's the Pixar way to understand very deeply what you are depicting.' And this aesthetic philosophy is crucial.

The film begins with the sound of Michael Giacchino's lively, French-inflected score and a whimsical rendition of the French national anthem, the *Marseillaise*.

The film's prologue is centred around a TV broadcast (*Up* begins similarly) which establishes food as being best in Paris and August Gusteau as the best chef in the city. There is then a cut to the archetypally harsh, demanding critic, Anton Ego, as he dismisses Gusteau's claim that anyone can cook. Ego retorts with the sneering comment: 'I don't think anyone can do it.' Immediately this film is established as being about the popular and ordinary versus the esoteric and elite. In effect, it's an echo of the idea that underpins *The Incredibles*.

There is then the sound of rainfall and we cut to a farmhouse on an autumnal day, the shot pushing in through the tree branches (the final shot of the film mirrors this with the camera pulling back to reveal Paris). A closer shot then moves in on one of the windows of the farmhouse and there is a freeze frame of Remy flying through the window with a cookbook in his hands. The film's (adult) voiceover begins (it's sort of redolent of Ray Liotta's voiceover in *GoodFellas* [Martin Scorsese, 1990]), Remy's voice suggesting a youthful character, the timbre of Patton Oswalt's vocal characterisation refreshingly alert. Remy's voiceover threads through the film, typically enhancing and adding to the action unfolding onscreen. Understandably enough, Remy lives with many other rats and spends much time with his brother Emile and their father who Remy tellingly introduces by saying, 'This is my dad. He's never impressed.' Surely that's a comment that many sons can relate to as part of the natural law that plays across the generations. Again, what we're really being told here is a story about human relationships. Remy talks with his dad and expresses frustration, noting of rats that, 'We're thieves, Dad.' There's such a sense of boredom and shame in this situation that you know Remy wants to do something about it. In part, this film is a father and son story about what it takes to forge your own path.

To varying degrees, Pixar films suggest a healthy awareness of some of the touchstones of film history and style. In this movie, once Remy arrives in Paris there's a real sense that he's akin to Gene Kelly's character in *An American In Paris* (Vincente Minnelli, 1951) in that both characters make their own lives anew in the City of Light.

Remy's motivation is made clear from the start of the film when he declares, in a mood of good-natured jealousy, that, 'Humans don't just survive, they discover, they create.' Alongside everything else, this is a film about being culturally educated. As he tries to explain to Emile the delights of food and its flavours, he munches on a strawberry and, at this moment, the filmmakers wow us with another film history nod: they invoke the abstract animation spirits of the great Norman McLaren and Oskar Fischinger to visualise Remy communicating his passions to Emile.

Only Emile knows that Remy has been hiding good food away to enjoy in his 'secret life', as Remy calls it.

Remy is a heroic character and an inventive one, too, making the flawed world work to his advantage. It's an attitude he adopts throughout the film and it's first seen at this early point when he turns a mushroom on a TV aerial over a flame. A storm then hits. Remy and Emile head inside the farmhouse and Remy decides he wants to get some saffron from the farmhouse kitchen. (Just look at the illusion of wooden texture on the spice rack and the detailed evocation of moss on the farmhouse walls.)

Remy reads quickly from the cookbook perched on the counter. This is fantastic: Remy is a movie hero who likes reading.

There is then a moment of destiny unfolding in unassuming surroundings as Remy sees Gusteau on the farmhouse TV. It becomes an epiphany for the bold-hearted rat. One shot pushes in on the TV screen to emphasise the import of what is showing and then there is a cut to Remy's reaction, the shot closing in on his awestruck little face.

Only Remy's brother Emile knows about Remy liking good food. Sometimes, though, one's passions can get the better of reason.

Gusteau inspires his TV audience with the statement that, 'The only limit is your soul. Anyone can cook, but only the fearless can be great.' We might say that this is a very American sensibility, the can-do attitude. Actually, it's worth noting what an optimistic film this is, a joyful one, actually; still the most joyful title that Pixar has yet produced.

We then learn that Gusteau died after a terrible Ego review (recalling the experience of David Lean, the film director, who was so shattered by negative reviews of *Ryan's Daughter* [1970] that he did not make another film for 12 years). Remy is shocked that Gusteau is dead. There isn't time to wallow in this, however, as the old lady who lives in the farmhouse sees Remy and Emile, chases them and shoots at them.

The comic timing when the old girl's rifle won't fire echoes the delightful moment in *The Incredibles* when the little boy on the trike watches Bob pick up the family car. It's as if time has momentarily frozen in order to attenuate the detail of that particular moment.

Remy just about escapes the farmhouse with the old lady's cookbook in his hands, but soon afterwards gets separated from his rat colony as they sail for a new home. It's a fateful moment and Remy finds himself alone in the sewers. We are given Remy's point of view of two tunnels forking off as he gets washed away. As Remy makes his way alone through the sewers, he holds Gusteau's book close to him and reads from it and, as he flicks the pages, the spirit of Gusteau speaks to him. We might even say that *Ratatouille* is *A Guy Named Joe* (Victor Fleming, 1943) with rats, and, with that in mind, it's absolutely the case that Gusteau is to Remy what Jiminy Cricket is to Pinocchio.

The ghost of Gusteau tells Remy to go and look around and, sure enough, Remy finds himself in a kitchen. Now the ghost appears alongside Remy, and he runs through Paris and on to a rooftop only to discover that he is in the place he dreamed of being: Paris.

We then follow Remy into Gusteau's restaurant and are introduced to a nervy-looking young man not wearing a chef's uniform. This is Alfredo Linguini and, in the tapestry of the story, he occupies the familiar role of the simple young man who is the butt of people's jokes, eventually rising to success and happiness. Kind-faced and somewhat startled-looking, he contrasts with the mean-spirited and mean-looking chef, Skinner, who has hired him as a garbage boy. The caricatured humans of the film have an almost Dickensian quality about them.

Remy, with the spirit of Gusteau alongside him, watches through the glass roof, their conversation guiding 'us' through the kitchen's process and the dynamics among the staff.

Remy watches as Alfredo meddles with the soup and, a moment later, falls into the kitchen and then frantically tries to get out. The breathless, floor-level camera pushing along as Remy flees takes us right back to the dynamics of the *Where the Wild Things Are* proof-of-concept sequence that John Lasseter and Glen Keane made in 1983 during their tenure at Disney as animators.

Remy sees Alfredo tasting the soup and, realising it needs improvement, adds some seasoning. Gusteau encourages Remy to really fix the soup, which he happily does. Alfredo then spies Remy on the edge of a saucepan and is both shocked and intrigued. Even though he's only trying to see Remy, Skinner thinks Alfredo is breaking kitchen hierarchy by doing some cooking, and he fires him immediately. However, when the food Remy has tweaked is given a good response by the food critic in the restaurant, the chef confronts Alfredo and asks, 'What are you playing at?' The other staff stand up for Gusteau's philosophy: he represents the common man and not the elite. Skinner decides to make the cook, Colette, responsible for Alfredo.

Skinner then spies Remy and goes after him, aiming to kill him. Alfredo catches Remy and removes him from the kitchen. Both at a low ebb, they make a connection as they take time out by the River Seine. And what a beautifully designed scene it is – just look at how the light from the lamps plays in the European fogginess. Spielberg's *The Adventures of Tintin* (2011) achieves the same degree of realism. Remy looks forlornly at Alfredo through the glass jar in which he is a prisoner. And then Alfredo realises that perhaps Remy could help him. He lets Remy out of the jar and they go back to Alfredo's rundown flat, which, despite its shabby condition, does offer a great view of Paris. Alfredo sleeps on the sofa and Remy looks out at Paris by night.

The next morning, Remy appears to be gone. But he's not. In fact, he's cooking, and there's the same sense of 'heroic return' in this little moment as in *Cars* when Lightning returns to Radiator Springs.

At Gusteau's, the staff read the review raving about the soup and the story now begins to turn on how Remy will help the restaurant get back on its feet, just as Lightning helps Radiator Springs revive its sense of self, and just as an adventure revives both Bob Parr in *The Incredibles* and Carl Fredricksen in *Up*.

Skinner then orders Alfredo to make the soup again and the pressure's really on. Alfredo and Remy work out how to communicate with each other as they train in Alfredo's apartment, and there's something of the quality of a silent film about this scene. People talk about *Wall E* as a silent film but this sequence in *Ratatouille* is equally well conjured.

Colette then talks to Alfredo and it's apparent that she is very driven, whereas Alfred is perhaps less so. In this way, Colette is not dissimilar to the equally resilient and strong Helen (aka Elastigirl in *The Incredibles*).

The buoyant comedy, farce even, of the story then shifts into plot developments of near-Dickensian dimensions as it's revealed that Skinner is making money from a frozen-food, ready-meal, spin-off business using Gusteau's name.

Furthermore, Gusteau's will comes to light and, in it, Alfredo is named as heir to the restaurant. The date given in the will means that Alfredo is due to take control of the restaurant four weeks hence and the story now has in place the race-against-time element that will propel the remainder of the narrative. Colette gives Alfredo more training in cooking and makes the critical point that the kitchen is a place of outsiders. This idea of the outsider characterises *The Incredibles* as well as Bird's non-Pixar film, *The Iron Giant*, which he made before working at Pixar. Then, too, Woody in *Toy Story* fears being rejected by Andy when Andy grows beyond childhood, and Nemo is very much an outsider for most of *Finding Nemo*.

The customers at the restaurant ask the waiter for something new and are brought the soup that Alfredo has made. (Just as *Cars* revelled in reflective surfaces and *A Bug's Life* in the colouring of an autumn leaf, this film delights in the fine mesh of the chef's hat which we see from Remy's point of view under the hat.) The customers love the dish that used to be a flop until Alfredo and Remy changed it. Alf is now the hero of the kitchen, whilst Skinner is jealous and angry about this turn of events. Jealousy is the root of many a bad guy's actions in Pixar movies: Randall Boggs in *Monsters, Inc*, Syndrome in *The Incredibles* and Muntz in *Up* come readily to mind.

Remy's brother Emile now turns up and then Remy's dad, too, who tries to get Remy to go back to the rat colony. However, Remy is reluctant to do so. In due course he does return home, albeit momentarily, but it's a necessary return in order for him to renew his resolve. The sequence captures something of that feeling you can experience when going back to the town you grew up in and it makes you realise just why you needed to move on.

As Remy's father puts it: 'We don't leave our nests, we make them bigger.' However, this isn't enough for Remy who replies, 'I'm tired of taking. I want to make things. I want to add something to this world.'

Remy's dad then takes Remy out and shows him the rat-trap shop, explaining that rats have to look out for themselves in a harsh world. Remy's retort, though, is to say that he doesn't believe that. Like Dash in *The Incredibles*, in the scene where he chats with his mother in the car about his powers, Remy must recognise that being different because of being gifted comes with its own set of complications. Remy is not a cynic and this is a very philosophical scene – unexpectedly insightful, perhaps, in delineating the different points that parents and their children must have. Remy's dad insists, 'You can't change nature,' to which Remy replies insistently that 'Change *is* nature, Dad.' This rather weighty conversation between Remy and his dad plays out in the rain, and the weather is important in that it heightens the sense of emotional instability, of things not being clear for Remy.

The next day, Remy finds Alfredo fast asleep in the kitchen and so tries to waken him; to animate him no less.

When Colette turns up for the day's work she finds that Alfredo is very tired. What she doesn't see is that Remy is controlling him.

Colette explains to Alfredo that she likes him but then loses her cool when she mistakes his tiredness for lack of interest in her. Alf then tells Colette that he loves her and, seizing the moment for big revelations, also explains about Remy's role in things. Alfredo and Colette kiss and the action cuts from the sweetness of blossoming romance to the ridiculous Anton Ego's office, styled like a cathedral to criticism, where Anton's assistant tells him that Gusteau's has regained popularity.

Ego is a skeletal figure with something cadaverous about him. In contrast to the heroes of the story, his sharp-angled body conveys nothing inviting, and it's worth noting here that the poses of the characters and their silhouettes make them immediately identifiable, economically saying something about their state of mind.

As time moves on, Skinner grows increasingly anxious about Alf. We then see Remy alone on the streets where people scream when they see him; once again, he's just another rat. 'I was reminded how the world saw me,' Remy confides in us, echoing what his dad has warned him about. His low point is compounded when Emile arrives at the restaurant with lots of other hungry rats in need of good food. Gusteau's ghost intervenes, very much in the spirit of Jiminy Cricket, to prod Remy's conscience with the question: 'They want you to steal?'

Remy gets a key that will allow him to unlock the food store. More importantly, he sees the will, and, it having been established at the very start of the film that he can read, quickly works out that Alfredo is the rightful owner of the restaurant. Remy runs off with the will and Skinner pursues him, eventually confronting Alfredo and Colette, who tells Skinner that his office is now rightfully Alfredo's.

Relentless in trying to stop Alfredo taking ownership, Skinner spies on the kitchen and calls a health inspector to tell him that the kitchen is rat infested. The stakes begin to mount as Anton Ego turns up and approaches Alfredo, telling him that he intends to return the next day to review the meals.

Skinner then realises that Remy is the cook. Nonetheless, Alfredo finds himself having to deal with new-found public and critical expectation about the restaurant (perhaps in the same position as a popular animation studio, we might say!).

Alfredo then sees that Remy is stealing food and kicks Remy out, too!

Remy returns to his dad, like the prodigal son, and admits defeat: 'You're right, Dad. Who am I kidding?'

Alfredo then addresses the cooks, whom Colette has told him he has to inspire. Remy is then caught by Skinner who wants Remy to make a new frozen-food recipe in exchange for Skinner's sparing his life.

Anton Ego arrives, ready to eat. Remy is in a cage and, just at the crucial moment, it's fathers to the rescue of their literal and figurative sons as both Gusteau's spirit and Remy's dad (and brother Emile) materialise to rescue Remy from his imprisonment.

Alf freaks out in the kitchen and then protects Remy when the chefs go for him with blades. Alf admits he has no talent and that the rat is the cook.

Most of the chefs walk out except for Colette, but then she goes, too. Meanwhile, Remy's father acknowledges his son's guts and all of the rats come to help out in the abandoned kitchen. Alf then sees them at work and the music underscoring the scene evokes Gershwin's 'An American In Paris'. To compose the music for the film, Brad Bird turned once again to Michael Giacchino with whom he had collaborated on *The Incredibles*. For this assignment, as Giacchino explained, he used a variety of different musical genres: 'There's European romanticism, quasi-classical music, a somewhat folk-pop song in it. It's got the most bizarre collection of influences that if you looked at them on paper, you'd go, "What, are you crazy? Pick one of these things but don't do them all."'[135]

Colette then returns to the kitchen and, in the restaurant, Ego eats a plate of ratatouille and is immediately transported back to a memory of his childhood and rustic happiness. Cooking is creativity and therefore good for the soul. Remy is then introduced to Ego and, in voiceover, we hear Ego offering the film's closing spoken words, which could be considered to be a thinly veiled comment about critics and criticism of any art form, particularly of popular art (movies come readily to mind, unsurprisingly). He says, 'In the grand scheme, a piece of junk is probably more meaningful than our criticism designating it so.'

The film's brief, all-visual coda begins with the camera pulling back from a kitchen window, echoing the very first shot of the film in which the camera pushed in on a farmhouse, and we see that Remy is now working in the kitchen of Alfredo's own place in Paris. It's a rather utopian conclusion of perfection and harmony: the ideal entertainment concoction and there's a real, earned sense of happily ever after.

Ahead of *Ratatouille*'s release there had been concerns over whether the title of the film would provide an impediment to commercial success. However, this wasn't to be the case. Certainly, it was seen as a total success and one of Pixar's most accomplished titles. Bird's creative dexterity with animation is particularly notable and we can only hope that, as of this writing, he is not for ever lost to the world of live-action films, as though they are somehow a more legitimate kind of filmmaking.

In his review of the film, Roger Ebert noted that 'A lot of animated movies have inspired sequels [...] but Brad Bird's is the first one that made me positively desire one.'[136] In the *Observer*, Philip French wrote that 'Pixar's *Ratatouille* is about education, aspiration, collaboration and challenging of stereotypes – a little gem that puts you in the right mood.'[137] And in the *San Francisco Chronicle* we could read that 'There are just enough slapstick moments to make the latest Pixar movie look, in the commercials, like a routine kid film, but it's something more complicated, and much more satisfying.'[138]

As a final bit of seasoning for this chapter it seems right to add a little here from *The Oxford Companion to Fairy Tales*, as it suggests a longer-running tradition of which *Ratatouille* is now a part: 'The romantics did not intend their fairy tales to amuse audiences in the traditional sense of *divertissement*. Instead, they sought to engage the reader in a serious discourse about art, philosophy, education and love. The focus was on the creative individual or artist who envisioned a life without inhibition and social constraints.'[139]

Wall-E (2008)

Directed by: Andrew Stanton
Written by: Andrew Stanton and Jim Reardon
Produced by: Jim Morris
Music by: Thomas Newman
Sound by: Ben Burtt
Edited by: Stephen Schaffer
Production Design: Ralph Eggleston
Art Direction: Anthony Christov
Visual Consulting: Roger Deakins and Dennis Muren
Cast: Ben Burtt (Wall-E), Elissa Knight (Eve), Jeff Garlin (Captain), Fred Willard (Shelby Forthright), Signourney Weaver (Ship's Computer)

American movies have a grand, longstanding tradition of vividly embracing the pleasures and insights offered by the bountiful science-fiction genre. *Wall-E* very much belongs to, and relishes being, a part of this heritage and genre. As a science-fiction film, then, *Wall-E* asks the fundamental question: 'What is it to be human?'

So, before doing anything else, let's start by considering the science-fiction genre, a set of storytelling patterns and views on the human condition that have been richly revised and tested over time.

Wall-E is distinctive for being the Pixar film with the longest sustained stretch without dialogue and, in approaching this aspect of the film, one could understand potential reticence on the part of the filmmakers in terms of how such a risk might affect the film's popularity. Ironically, though, the more dialogue-free a film is, the stronger it might be, not mired in the potential ordinariness of realistic dialogue and unhampered by the barriers of spoken language. Images have a universality about them. Sometimes, arresting visuals can be quickly flattened and devalued by ponderous dialogue that aims for realism. This is where George Lucas succeeded with the dialogue for the *Star Wars* prequels: their absence of everyday cadence was consistent with the grandiose nature of the settings and situation. It's more in keeping with the poetry (not in the sense of rhyme, but of article) of Greek dramatic language. Robert Bresson, whose own films are pretty much the opposite of Pixar in every way, said of plot and 'traditional' drama in relation to cinema: 'Dramatic stories should be thrown out. They have nothing whatsoever to do with cinema […] It seems to me that when one tries to do something dramatic with film, one is like a man who tries to hammer with a saw. Film would have been marvellous if there hadn't been dramatic art to get in the way.'[140]

Critical to the realisation of *Wall-E* was a powerful emphasis on its soundtrack. Certainly, animation and sound (representational and non-representational) have a rich history of working together and Walter Murch has noted of the relationship that 'film sound is rarely appreciated for itself alone, but functions largely as an enhancement of the visual'.[141] Of his work on the film, Burtt commented that:

> I suppose I could have hired actors and had them stand in front of a mike and recorded their voices and dubbed that in over character action, but that would have of course not taken the whole idea of the illusion very far. What he wanted was the illusion that these robot characters, the speech and sounds they made, were really coming from their functions as machines, that there was either a chip on board that synthesised the voice or the squeak of their motor would sound cute, and that would give an indication how they feel. The problem does go back, for me, to the sort of primal R2-D2 idea, which is how do you have a character not speak words or, in the case of Wall-E, just a very few words, but you understand what is going on in their head and they also seem to have a depth of character. So it is a matter of that relationship, how much electronic, how much human, and you sway back and forth to create the different sounds.[142]

The film's conceptual art testifies to the depth of development and consideration and working out of the logic of Wall-E the robot. A particularly arresting piece of conceptual art for the film is to be found in Jay Shuster's engineering drawing of all of Wall-E's parts, as though he were a product you could buy and assemble.

As a science-fiction film, *Wall-E* gives expression to a range of necessary and familiar generic tropes. Writing about science fiction, the scholar J P Telotte has noted that the genre 'has become associated with both the internal life of the mind and an external world of otherness, the not-mind'[143].

Wall-E features two songs from *Hello, Dolly!* (Gene Kelly, 1969) – 'Put On Your Sunday Clothes' and 'It Only Takes A Moment' – and they function as motifs that symbolise the overarching themes of the film. Of the production design, Ralph Eggleston commented that the work of designer/architect Santiago Calatrava was key to his aesthetic, noting that 'I love how he organises organic forms into beautifully patterned structures. It's so futuristic and yet very comforting as well.'[144]

Wall-E begins with an image of a starscape. It is beautiful, an image that reflects our boundless inner space of the mind and deepest atomic being, and it is gloriously and frustratingly unfathomable. A little unexpectedly, we hear a song from *Hello, Dolly!* playing (quite in contrast to the grandiose, sombre or fanfare-inflected music we might typically associate with such a setting in a film) and it's a witty juxtaposition with the hard-to-fathom ultra-enormity of space. We move in towards the wasteland of our earth and descend through the clouds towards terra firma, where we see immense windmills and a desolate land. It's a classic, post-apocalyptic realm and it's utterly believable and photorealistic. Indeed, there's nothing as yet on screen to announce that we are watching an animated film. We might expect to see Max Rockatansky down there. The cheery musical track continues to play, making the setting all the more eerie. An overhead shot sweeps us low over the derelict city and the song slowly fades to an echo. An overhead shot then provides the first view of the robot, Wall-E, moving far, far below. We watch him from above and then from ground level as he goes about his work; a tiny fragment of activity in an immense, and essentially static, world.

As Wall-E goes about the place, a little cockroach is present (it might remind some of you of the bug in Jeff Smith's comic series, *Bone*). Gesture and sounds drive the action and it's compelling.

Haunting music is heard as the 'camera' pulls back to reveal the enormity of the dead world (which we will learn is Earth, of course). Everyone appears to have gone: a fact that's clarified soon after. We learn through what we see that it was a consumer world. The camera tracks along and we see huge city structures, with tiny Wall-E moving amongst them. He goes to a defunct terminal and we see a hologram showing the Axiom space vessel heading for space. This briefly presented piece of information is all the backstory we need. Critically, the hologram image shows us a population that looks in good health.

The camera zooms in and hunts out Wall-E in a way that evokes the quality of a vérité documentary film picking out a detail in a larger context. We are then shown Wall-E's home in a big old storage truck. Like Gene Kelly in *An American In Paris* (Vincente Minnelli, 1951) he has made a comfortable home out of very little, pretty with the colour of the fairy lights. It's a self-sufficiency that rhymes with the way that Remy builds a life for himself in the kitchen of *Ratatouille*. Wall-E is a hoarder and he watches *Hello, Dolly!* on an iPod and magnifies it with a sheet of magnifying glass. Wall-E's got the inventive spark of a human and eyes as expressive as any of his fellow Pixar heroes.

We're quick to notice that the movie clip Wall-E watches is the only vibrant, bright colour in his brown, burnished world, and he loses himself in the love story of the film. Wall-E looks up at the stars and a storm whoops up and he takes cover. He's rather like a castaway.

The next day an immense ship lands and it's rather 'classic' in its sleek form. He meets Eve, a new robot, who Wall-E watches, cocking his head like a curious puppy. Certainly, Wall-E's 'face' is entirely composed of his eyes and it prompts us to consider the longstanding idea about babies/eyes/headsize eliciting our sympathy. Eve resembles an Apple product with her curvilinear form. (As an aside, Steve Jobs studied calligraphy at Reed College in Oregon and acknowledged that this influenced his stylistic sensibilities.)

Wall-E and Eve befriend each other and she flies around, delighting in the new landscape that she is exploring. As she bonds with Wall-E, it rather recalls the particular scenes of bonding between ET and Elliott in *ET: The Extra-Terrestrial* (Steven Spielberg, 1982) when Elliot talks ET through his toy collection.

Another storm comes and Wall-E takes Eve to the safety of his home, and the camera pushes in on her as she looks up at the pretty lights. Wall-E dances and so does Eve, but she's a bit too powerful. Soon afterwards, the robots' reverie is interrupted when Eve's base ship returns to collect her. Wall-E bravely jumps aboard the ship, holding on to its exterior, and there's a shot that mimics the position taken by cameras on the exterior of NASA ships when they have launched, the world falling rapidly away beneath their trajectory.

Wall-E rides above the earth and there is a momentary sense of peace and calm all around. Wall-E then gets aboard the Axiom, stowaway that he is, and explores the ship, seeing its countless overweight passengers, including their captain. A series of shots shows how banal life for the people on the ship is and this makes for a soft-edged critique of the insulated lives that so many of us find ourselves living. It's a moment that reminds us of the connection between animation and caricature; a relationship at the heart of animation's ability to criticise, amplify and subvert.

The captain then looks at Eve and determines that she has come back with a positive result, indicated by the little green plant icon light on her body. Eve has returned with a specimen, the evidence that photosynthesis is working again on Earth. This means that the humans can therefore now return to Earth if it's restoring itself to health.

The Captain is so overweight that his hands are no longer nimble enough to open a book with. Meanwhile, Eve finds that Wall-E is a stowaway and the Captain initiates a procedure to open Eve up to get the plant. In a well-integrated science-fiction movie reference, the red light that occupies the Captain's chamber recalls HAL in *2001* (Stanley Kubrick, 1969).

It might be reasonable to suggest here that Wall-E's adventures around the Axiom lack the storytelling intrigue and invention of the earthbound action. Where that material was lyrical and suffused with a sense of mystery and surprise, this part of the film is more manic and familiar to us. Nonetheless, for all of the slapstick hijinks, the story continues to offer more openly emotional moments and it's rather affecting to realise that both Wall-E and Eve are effectively fugitives on board the ship. Indeed, rather like Boo in *Monsters, Inc*, they are potentially contaminating the sealed world they have ventured into illegally. As they rush and rocket around the Axiom's corridors and chambers there's certainly much to be enjoyed in terms of the lighting and decor of these spaces as they echo various classic science-fiction design statements. Identified as 'contaminating' elements aboard the antiseptic, pristine ship, Wall-E and Eve in a way represent spontaneous action and energy far exceeding that of the numbed and slothful humans. Indeed, there's something of the sensibility of the cult science-fiction films like *THX 1138* (George Lucas, 1971) and *Silent Running* (Douglas Trumbull, 1972) in the film at this point. It's certainly a movie that's aware of its genre antecedents. Eventually, Wall-E and Eve's adventures within the ship lead them back out, and one of the film's most charming scenes ensues in which the two dance amongst the stars in a way that emphasises the tenderness of their relationship, and especially their sense of humour.

Getting back on board, Eve confronts the ship's Captain who she knows has hidden the plant specimen that she brought back from earth. Sure enough, the Captain realises that it is time for everyone to return to Earth as there is life in evidence again. Revived by Eve's gift, the Captain makes the point that 'I don't want to survive. I want to live.'

Wall-E and Eve then set about taking the ship back home to Earth where, upon arrival, the film moves towards its climax. Wall-E appears to be dead, in a turn of events that nicely rhymes with another science-fiction love story, *ET: The Extra Terrestrial*, and Eve takes him home and resuscitates him and fixes him with new parts. However, these new parts mean that he doesn't quite remember the things that meant something to him before leaving Earth. Would you believe it? Here we are at the end of the movie and the grandest statement of all, about identity, is being made without recourse to speech. Wall-E doesn't even respond to his cherished film, *Hello, Dolly!* At this tense moment, the emotional intensity of the scene plays out significantly in Eve's expressive blue eyes. There is then silence as Eve holds Wall-E's hand, her digits rather evocative of Apple products and Wall-E's very much of an older, mechanical world. As he holds Eve's hand, Wall-E begins to remember. As with *Up*, it's memory that proves the real source of strength for the beleaguered hero. Wall-E is alive again and no longer alone.

Having made a film in *Finding Nemo* about the love of a father and son for each other, and a journey far from the comforts and certainties of home, the writer-director Andrew Stanton developed *Wall-E* from an original concept that had its origins many years before:

> There was this lunch we had during *Toy Story* around '94 and we were batting around any idea we could think of to come up with what the next movie could be. One of the half brained sentences was that we could do a sci-fi thing where we had the last robot on earth. Everybody has left and this machine didn't know it could stop and it keeps doing it forever. That's really where it started. All the details weren't there. There wasn't a name for the character. We didn't know what it would look like. It was just the loneliest scenario I'd ever heard and I just loved it. I think that's why it stayed in the ether for so long.[145]

The film loses a little of its simplicity and impact once Wall-E and Eve find themselves on board the immense space cruiser and the film moves from its Buster Keaton/Charlie Chaplin-informed 'action' movie to something closer in spirit to the physicality of a Chuck Jones animated short. Amidst the race and chase of the film's second part, however, the film still provides lyrical pauses in the action.

Roger Ebert called *Wall-E* 'an enthralling animated film, a visual wonderment and a decent science fiction story'[146]. In the UK's *Empire* magazine they called it '[Pixar's] most ambitious undertaking since *Toy Story*'[147]. Intergalactic fantastic though *Wall–E* may be, this little hero is really just a highly evolved version of the charming Tinny from the early Pixar short, *Tin Toy* (1988).

Up (2009)

Directed by: Pete Docter
Co-directed by: Bob Peterson
Written by: Pete Docter and Bob Peterson
Produced by: Jonas Rivera
Music by: Michael Giacchino
Sound by: Tom Myers
Edited by: Kevin Nolting
Production Design: Ricky Nierva
Cast: Ed Asner (Carl Fredricksen), Christopher Plummer (Charles Muntz), Jordan Nagai (Russell), Bob Peterson (Dug), Delroy Lindo (Beta), Jerome Ranft (Gamma), Bob Peterson (Alpha)

In 1921, American animator and illustrator Winsor McCay produced a film entitled *The Flying House*, the creation of which is also credited to his son, Robert. In 2011, this short film was restored by the animator Bill Plympton who said of his major restoration project:

> In 1921, Winsor McCay created one of his greatest short films, *The Flying House*. Unfortunately for animation history, his boss William Randolph Hearst felt that the talented artist was neglecting his drawing duties at the paper, and demanded that he stop making films. So, sadly, *The Flying House* was McCay's last film. Who knows what great achievements he could have attained had he not given up his animation career. With his talent, he could have surpassed Walt Disney, whose Mickey Mouse was still six years in the future.[148]

As an aside, McCay is so iconic and important to visual culture that Google, on 14 October 2012, uploaded a Google Doodle to celebrate his birthday.

The Flying House is a fitting starting point in considering Pete Docter's film *Up*. Interestingly, and perhaps most famously, the idea of a flying house also spins into view in the opening of L Frank Baum's *The Wonderful Wizard of Oz* as Dorothy is transported from Kansas via a tornado that lifts the family home skyward. Then, too, the children's author Chris Van Allsburg set his story *Zathura* in a suburban house as it flies through outerspace. And there is also Hayao Miyazaki's adaptation of Diana Wynne Jones' novel, *Howl's Moving Castle*. And what about the excellent, albeit relatively little seen, demonstration of performance capture, *Monster House*. This image of the flying house resonates so readily because of how it embodies that sense of breaking free from the ordinariness and routine of experience that is necessary, but which sometimes we might wish to escape. As such, it becomes an emblem of what movies themselves can accomplish for us.

The adventure genre, of which *Up* is such a fine example, poses the tough-minded question: 'Are you good enough?' The adventure genre includes movies such as the *Indiana Jones* quartet, *The Last of the Mohicans* (Michael Mann, 1992), *The Searchers* (John Ford, 1956) or *Lord of the Rings: The Fellowship of the Ring* (Peter Jackson, 2001). It might sound a little too much, but one of the fascinations of *Up*, when its title was announced, was its brevity and graphic appeal. Indeed, for the extended period before any artwork or screen image was released, there was enough to spark the imagination in just the emblem of a house suspended beneath countless balloons. It became an image that spoke not only of the film's premise, but also something broader: of elevating the mundane through fantastic means. To make the ordinary extraordinary and show us things afresh is what the best films can achieve.

Just as we might see *Ratatouille* and *Toy Story* as reworkings of stories such as *The Elves and the Shoemaker*, *Up* can be considered a reimagining of the classic novel by Miguel de Cervantes, *Don Quixote* (1605). The Quixote story is central to the development of the novel and has been repeatedly referenced and invoked and reworked, so why not for movies, too? Of Don Quixote, Harold Bloom has said that 'Cervantes plays upon the human need to withstand suffering, which is one reason the knight awes us. However good a Catholic he may (or may not) have been, Cervantes is interested in heroism and not in sainthood.'[149] This recycling, reforming and reinterpretation keeps the storytelling tree alive and well.

Alongside its literary antecedents, *Up* also evidences the significant impact of George Lucas and Steven Spielberg's films. These two producers made a number of feature films in the 1970s and 1980s that achieved great popularity and which often centred on very ordinary young characters adventuring beyond their own homes to discover great things, both outside and within themselves. Their adventures were not without risk and danger, and so they always proved enriching.

In discussing the development and conceptual work of Pete Docter, acknowledgement has been made of the influence of producer and director Jim Henson. Henson had died at an early age in May 1990. Since the 1960s his name had become synonymous with his puppet creations, most famously The Muppets, and his involvement with the vanguard educational programme, *Sesame Street*. As a director on two 'cult' fantasy films, *The Dark Crystal* (1982) and *Labyrinth* (1986), Henson is well and kindly remembered. Henson's work as a producer emphasised humour and also a real humanist warmth. There was nothing nihilistic in his work and, whilst he always acknowledged the sad side of life, his characters embodied a genuine sense of hope, both in ourselves and in others, that endures. This warmth, for want of a better term, underpins both *Up* and *Monsters, Inc*, and, by extension, Pixar's other movies and short films.

Up's visual style has a high-key brightness akin to that which we see in Docter's previous film, *Monsters, Inc*. Like that film, *Up* is about the power of storytelling. Where *Monsters, Inc* emphasised the power of humour, however, *Up* emphasises the power of memory.

The character of Carl Fredricksen is the antithesis of who we might typically expect to be the centre of an action-adventure movie and, like so many animated characters, he has also come to live outside of the film as a merchandised image which, apart from generating profit for the producer and studio, embeds the emotional resonance and 'meaning' of the story more deeply in the popular culture. Carl's performance is defined in large part by his facial expressions and, as with *The Incredibles* and *Ratatouille*, the human designs are relatively abstract – there's no attempt at realism.

The film begins with a much-lauded prologue that seems to have reminded many of cinema's roots in silent film, where there's no recourse to the potential clutter of dialogue.

In keeping with the example of *The Incredibles* and *Ratatouille*, and the dramatic device of foreshadowing later action, *Up* begins with a newsreel footage sequence seeding story elements that will pay off much later: Movietown news, in the form of a 1930s newsreel piece, provides the film's backstory, showing footage of a lost jungle world. There's certainly a King Kong vibe about the material, and the music we hear accompanying the prologue is Muntz's theme, which composer Michael Giacchino has described thus: 'I wanted his theme to start out as this really kind of innocent, new world kind of thing. It's a celebratory theme.'[150]

The news story focuses on the young adventurer Charles Muntz (is this a riff on the name Charles Mintz, the film distributor who had distributed Walt Disney's *Oswald the Lucky Rabbit* films in the 1920s?) and his year-long expedition to find a mythical jungle bird. The sequence cuts from the newsreel footage to a close-up of a boy named Carl Fredricksen. He is wearing an aviator's helmet and goggles as he watches the newsreel footage wide-eyed. We hear the 'adventure is out there' musical motif as the newsreel continues, explaining that Muntz returned to the USA with a monster skeleton but was accused of its being fake and subsequently stripped of his honours. Muntz returned to the lost world, promising to capture the monster of Paradise Falls. The prologue then dissolves to Carl playing on his neighbourhood street with the newsreel narrator's voice now momentarily narrating Carl's own suburban adventure. Fleetingly, reality and fantasy have merged.

In close-up, we see Carl as he stops, hearing a girl's voice emanating from a tumbledown house and proclaiming that 'Adventure is out there!' Carl goes into the abandoned house to find a little girl about his age playing there. Her name is Ellie. She pretends to pilot the house (an apparently incidental action which will take on a critical weight later in the film when things are all too real). The images of the children playing suggest something of the visual influence of Norman Rockwell and also of the comic strip, *Peanuts*, and the *Little Rascals* movie series of the 1940s.

As Ellie plays, very much for her own satisfaction, she befriends Carl, who says very little. Carl is then shown in bed at home and Ellie arrives at his window under night skies. Indeed, the balloon motif prompts a connection with the movie *The Red Balloon* (Albert Lamorisse, 1956) and there's something very much in the spirit of Tom Sawyer in Ellie's energy. Ellie talks a lot, contrary to Carl, and we realise that we're in something akin to rom-com territory. Ellie shows Carl her adventure book and tells of her dream to go and live in Paradise Falls (Paradise Falls being what happens when childhood passes for all of us). In a near matching and bridging of sound, a balloon bursts and becomes the sound of a flashbulb firing as Carl and Ellie's wedding photo is taken.

The sequence continues with Carl and Ellie seeing their dream home and Ellie, still in her wedding dress, doing DIY. It's a moment conjuring a film reference that might be a little esoteric for the contemporary young audience: *It's A Wonderful Life* (Frank Capra, 1946) comes to mind in the shot of Ellie fixing up the house in her wedding clothes. We then see Carl and Ellie playfully putting their paint-caked handprints on their postbox. Indeed, the postbox in this film becomes a prop invested with meaning equalled only by the emotional power emanating from the postbox in the film adaptation of the novel *The Color Purple*. With only music playing over the sequence charting their life together, we watch Carl and Ellie cloudbusting. This sequence is a high-key, low-contrast series of images that brim with a sense of happiness. As such, the one moment in the sequence that's an exception to the overall style is when a grey colour palette is applied for the tableau image of Ellie and Carl when they are at the doctor's and they realise that they will not be able to have children. The action then cuts to Ellie alone and sad. Carl brings her the adventure book and we see them begin saving for Paradise Falls.

We then see the couple dancing in older age. Carl picks up a picture of Ellie as a little girl and looks sad. Time is passing. He then goes and buys Peru tickets. A brief tableau set at sundown shows Ellie falling ill. The sunset colour suggests something of the late stage in life that Ellie and Carl have reached.

Ellie dies and, instead of this event being shown, we see Carl alone on the step of a church altar with a funeral wreath at his side. This choice to allude to an event – to include the audience in completing the puzzle, if you like – occurs at other points in the film and makes for a satisfying conversation between film and audience.

The action then cuts to Carl waking up, a wide shot used to show him getting out of bed and going about his morning routine. His loneliness is what we come to experience very quickly in a little sequence that almost feels like a film directed by Yasujiro Ozu. Indeed, *Up* is about the passing of time just as Ozu's widely acknowledged classic, *Tokyo Story* (1953), is. Who'd have thought we'd be talking about Ozu and Pixar in the same sentence? That said, Michael Arndt, screenwriter for *Toy Story 3*, has acknowledged that his favourite film is Ozu's *Late Spring* (1949).

Touchingly, even in old age, Carl still wears the grape-soda badge that Ellie gave him when they were kids. There is then an abrupt cut to reveal Carl's house amidst a demolition site. It's an image that might recall a similar shot in the fantasy film *batteries not included* (Matthew Robbins, 1987), in which an elderly couple have an extraordinary encounter. Defiant that he won't move from his imperilled house, Carl takes a nap. It's at this point that there is a knock on the door. Carl opens it to find a Boy Scout, Russell, standing there. As in *The Incredibles*, the hands express much about a character's state of mind and response to a situation. As Russell talks endlessly, just look at Carl's hands as he puts them to his face in despair. Carl returns indoors and it seems that he is indeed going to move on to Shady Oaks retirement home. Quietly looking through Ellie's Adventure Book, he sees a picture of Paradise Falls and crosses his heart. This tender moment then cuts to another day and a man from the Shady Oaks retirement home pulls up to take Carl away. Instead, and without any advance information for the audience, a cloud of multicoloured balloons emerges through the chimney of Carl's house and the building breaks free of the earth (literally and metaphorically for Carl). It's a joyful moment and there's a fleetingly lyrical moment when the wash of colour thrown by the balloons passes over the wall of a little girl's bedroom. Michael Giacchino's score is emphatically waltz-like for this moment, as though Carl and Ellie continue to dance together in memory. This is a film about little grace-notes of beauty.

The sequence then cuts to an image of a map of South America as the house embarks on its globetrotting flight. Humorously, Carl sits quietly in his chair. A wide shot then shows us the fragile little house up above the clouds where all is silent. And THEN! There is a knock at the door. Carl discovers that Russell is still on the porch. The momentum of the action builds and there's a drama-enhancing detail of the balloon strings in the fireplace trembling. Something's happening and a cut to outside the house shows it entering a storm in a moment that's an overt reference to the film's *Wizard of Oz* (Victor Fleming, 1939) connection. In *Toy Story*, Oz gets a reference, too, as Woody races to escape Sid's haunting house. Like *The Wizard of Oz*, *Up* sees its protagonist having to go away from home in order to find out exactly what it means to them.

The action then cuts to the next day and the point of view of Carl and Russell is shown as several towering rock formations whoosh by with eerie force at the edge of the frame. There then follows a bit of action business that culminates in an actual cliffhanger for Carl, Russell and the house as a rainbow elegantly arcs through the mist of the Falls.

Already, the film has tapped into the rich vein of silent film comedy. As a narrative device it's made clear that Carl and Russell have three days to reach the Falls before the helium that holds up the house runs out. The story now has a ticking-clock scenario, a race against time shaping the ensuing part of the story as Carl and Russell trek through the beautiful wilderness, its density of foliage and richness of colour recalling paintings by Henri Rousseau such as 'Surprised!' (1891).

The action then cuts to Russell following the tracks of a big bird he subsequently names Kevin. Russell and Carl then discover a dog named Dug who functions similarly to Dory in *Finding Nemo*.

The film allows plenty of opportunity for us to enjoy the details of the animation; just look at how the dogs breathe and look, too, at how the production design detail so accurately creates the illusion of light spilling around the edge of the rocks and between the jungle foliage. Carl and Russell camp out on a rainy night, rain being significant in movies, typically adding to the sense of emotional uncertainty and unease. Just look at the use of rain in *Ratatouille* and *Toy Story 3*. Like Remy and his father conversing in *Ratatouille*, Carl and Russell's conversation really allows them to understand each other. Of rain in the movies, the film scholar Jim Kitses has written that 'like fog and mist, rain is symbolic weather that represents an intensification of noir's darkness (its "murk"), the shadow world rendered not only mysterious and dangerous but destabilising, turbulent, hostile'[151]. The expressive detail in this fireside scene is notable. Russell looks forlorn and doesn't look directly at Carl whose eyes register his sadness at hearing Russell's story.

Another day dawns and Carl's face is now showing stubble in a nice storytelling detail. As the boy and the old man doggedly advance, we've a real sense of the idea of the explorer in the wilderness – in alien territory, we might say – that ties the film to the work of Jules Verne, Edgar Rice Burroughs and even to the Werner Herzog film *Fitzcarraldo* (1982). Carl and Russell are led by a pack of dogs into the ravine from where Muntz emerges (Kurtz-like!) from shadow into just the most delicate of beams of light; we can just about see him. He is indeed like Kurtz in *Apocalypse Now* (Francis Ford Coppola, 1979), a self-made king in the wilderness, far from civilisation.

Carl's expression when he realises that he is now standing face to face with his now very aged childhood hero captures awe and delight. Indeed, the idea of hero-worship and how it can skew echoes a key story point that's fundamental to *The Incredibles*. Muntz shows Carl the monster skeletons, after which they have dinner. Muntz's obsession with finding the bird, which Carl and Russell have easily located, compels him in very negative ways. Tellingly, Carl and Russell have found the bird by showing him kindness.

Muntz quickly emerges as the villain of the piece and, when Carl recognises that Muntz isn't the nice guy of legend, the moment of revelation occurs in low-key lighting conditions. Muntz is shadowy and of the shadows. Muntz then sees Kevin on the house and Carl and Russell make a break for freedom. They just about get away but Kevin is hurt during the chase. Russell puts a bandage on Kevin and Carl agrees they'll get Kevin home to his nest. Amusingly, notes Russell, 'the wilderness isn't quite what I expected'. It's a funny line but it makes me think of Michael Chabon's essay in which he ruminates on kids and the wild: 'What is the impact of the closing down of the Wilderness on the development of children's imaginations? This is what I worry about the most. I grew up with a freedom, a liberty that now seems breathtaking and almost impossible.'[152]

The voice of experience, Carl says you have to get used to things not being as you expect. The collision of fantasy and reality that had been rather sweet in that moment at the beginning of the film, when Carl met Ellie, now assumes an uneasy quality. Russell makes a particularly astute comment about memory when he explains that 'I think the boring stuff is the stuff I remember most'.

Just as they think they're arrived back at Kevin's nest, Muntz nets the bird and then sets fire to the house. We see a picture of Ellie on the wall of the front room as it falls and smashes. As Kevin is put on board an airship, Carl douses the fire and saves the house, but now finds himself at his lowest ebb, saying, 'I didn't ask for any of this.'

One of the most arresting images of the film then occurs, echoing the use of silhouette and reddening skies to mark a low point in an earlier part of the film. This time we see the house in silhouette against a deep red sky (almost like the red of a Mark Rothko painting), a lyrical image that's suffused with a touch of tragedy. However, as Carl goes back into the damaged house, he finds himself unexpectedly re-energised through an act of memory and of love. Elsewhere in this book we've referred to the impact of Spielberg's movies on the generation of Pixar directors currently working at the studio and there is something Spielbergian in this moment that recalls scenes in *Hook* (1991) and *Amistad* (1997) and also the Spielberg production, *Casper* (Brad Silberling, 1995). Carl resets the furniture in the room and we are reminded of the film's early shots when we were introduced to Carl in the quiet routine of life at home. Once again, we see him sitting in his armchair and it's as though the adventure has not happened. Carl looks through Ellie's adventure book as Giacchino's score is played on a wistful piano. He sees pictures of home life in the adventure book – that's the adventure! This is rather like Helen seeing home life as the adventure. Is this not, though, a very conservative attitude, in that it's the man who gets the larger-than-life adventure whilst woman has to settle for domesticity? Ellie could just as easily have been the one going to the jungle.

Carl is renewed emotionally and spiritually by his quiet moment alone and, when he resumes his involvement with the adventure, he sees that Russell has gone to rescue Kevin from the airship. Carl literally rejects his past at this point so as to move on; in very pragmatic terms he needs to lighten the load of the house, and there's an amusing and potent image of Carl and Ellie's old armchairs abandoned on the rocks of Paradise Falls. The race against time kicks in with new urgency now.

A dynamic air battle, as kinetically charged as the door vault chase at the close of *Monsters, Inc*, ensues, with a literal 'dogfight' taking place as Muntz's hounds pilot biplanes. Carl now finds himself truly in the midst of the kind of larger-than-life adventure he dreamed of as a child. He has become the hero. Carl even ends up swashbuckling with Muntz and there's what seems to be an homage to a shot in *Indiana Jones and the Temple of Doom* (Steven Spielberg, 1984) when Muntz falls down the ladder on the exterior of the airship. It echoes the moment when Mola Ram tumbles down the rope ladder as he brawls with Indiana Jones. Muntz falls to his doom. The house then falls through clouds to its end (coming to rest for 'eternity' on Paradise Falls). Russell and Carl pilot the airship home. Russell gets his Wilderness badge and Carl is there for him. A little epilogue then follows in which we see Carl and Russell on a suburban sidewalk sharing an ice cream.

As with each of Pixar's other films, the kinetic action, humour, and tension are counterpointed by lyrical, quieter moments. The emblematic image of the house in flight above the parcels of land that speak of rural America and the Midwest tap into a real-world sensibility that anchors the Pixar fantasies. In this lyrical attitude there's a nod, too, to the films of Hayao Miyazaki, whose work has become relatively well known in Europe and America and has often been referenced by Pixar as an accomplished example of the animated form.

In his review of the film, Roger Ebert wrote that '*Up* tells a story as tickling to the imagination as the magical animated films of my childhood, when I naively thought that, because their colours were brighter, their character outlines more defined and their plots simpler, they were actually more realistic than regular films'[153]. *Time Out* observed that the film was 'not to be confused with the Russ Meyer/Roger Ebert bongo classic'[154], whilst *Empire*'s verdict was that 'if it had lived up to its golden first five minutes, *Up* would have been the film of the decade'[155].

In her book *Boys and Girls Forever*, Alison Lurie makes an observation that in fact strikes at the heart of *Up*'s storytelling power when she explains that European fairy tales see people change whilst the world around them stays the same. In the American mode, the world changes or even falls away[156] and Lurie brings into play here Carl Sandburg's 'Rootabaga' stories. Lurie adds that 'in American fairy tales there is often not much to be said for wealth and high position'[157].

Elsewhere in this book we've talked about the Pixar/Dr Seuss connection and Alison Lurie has made a point about Seuss that relates very clearly to *Up*: 'Innovative as he was, Seuss can also be seen as squarely in the tradition of American popular humour. His [...] energy and delight in invention and nonsense recall the boasts and exaggeration of the nineteenth-century tall tale.'[158]

So Carl and Russell embody the supremely American character of Huckleberry Finn, from Mark Twain's novel *The Adventures of Huckleberry Finn* (1884/5), who yearns to 'light out for the territory'[159] and be apart from the demands of civilisation.

In *Up*, Carl learns the lesson that your heroes can let you down, but, in turn, as you grow up, you become your own hero based on the gathering of life experience. Heroes for kids give them the experiences that they just can't have as young people.

Finally, a comment from a writer whose life long predated *Up* and who could not have come from a more different situation. And yet… something he wrote fits perfectly with the experience that Carl Fredricksen has in the movie. Here's the French philosopher Gaston Bachelard, in his book *The Poetics of Space*, on the subject of houses. 'If I were asked to name the chief benefit of the house I should say: the house shelters daydreaming, the house protects the dreamer, the house allows us to dream in peace.'[160]

Toy Story 3 (2010)

Directed by: Lee Unkrich
Written by: Michael Arndt (screenplay), Andrew Stanton, John Lasseter and Lee Unkrich (story)
Produced by: Darla K Anderson
Music by: Randy Newman
Edited by: Ken Schretzmann
Cast: Tom Hanks (Woody Pride), Tim Allen (Buzz Lightyear), Don Rickles (Mr Potato Head), Michael Keaton (Ken), Ned Beatty (Lotso)

One of the pleasures to be taken from a series of movies, connected by returning characters and ongoing storylines, is the sense of a journey being made, not only by the characters in the film but also, no doubt, by some in the audience, too. When a film series spans more than a decade there's a powerful sense of time having passed.

Certainly, movie trilogies are plentiful across the genres, but only a small number of these series or serials cohere and sustain their storytelling interest. We might think of Coppola's majestic *Godfather* trilogy, the octet of *Harry Potter* films, the frantic *Back to the Future* trilogy, Sergio Leone's spaghetti western trilogy or even Satyajit Ray's *Apu* films. And we can now add to this list the achievement of the *Toy Story* trilogy. With *Toy Story 3*, Pixar capped a sequence of films that have embedded themselves in popular culture and become a benchmark for affecting, computer-animated filmmaking.

For all the creative and commercial happy endings surrounding *Toy Story 3*, its beginning was less auspicious, which may seem odd given the success of *Toy Story* and *Toy Story 2*. However, once the Pixar-Disney deal had been renegotiated, *Toy Story 3* remained on the production schedule and moved towards its summer 2010 release date. Here's Lee Unkrich delineating the situation in which the film began to be developed:

> Bob Iger, Disney chief at the time, had only wanted Pixar staff to be involved in making the film. One of the reasons for the delay was the troubled relationship Pixar had with Disney before a $7.4 billion deal made them corporate cousins in 2006. There was a lot of friction between the two companies that kept us from making the film. We had a five-picture deal with Disney at the time, and sequels to [earlier] films didn't count towards that deal. So it was kind of a stalemate. Disney ended up using the idea of *Toy Story 3* as kind of a bargaining chip, and, unfortunately, they started making their own version against our wishes. Pixar hasn't really had many dark times in its history, but that was probably the darkest time when their version of *Toy Story 3* was being made because these were our characters, these were our children and they had been kind of taken away from us. No one was happy about it. Fortunately, that alternate version of the future never came to be because [current Disney president] Bob Iger took over, and one of his first orders of business was to negotiate and ultimately purchase Pixar, which finally freed us up to make our own version of *Toy Story 3*.[161]

Of the third film's development, its director Lee Unkrich (who had co-directed *Toy Story 2* with John Lasseter) said of its conceptual stage: 'At the end of *Toy Story 2*, Woody acknowledges that Andy is going to grow up some day, and he seems to make peace with that fact. But, as we all know, in real life, making peace with something that's going to happen way off in the abstract future is quite different from finding yourself on that day having to deal with it.'[162]

Michael Arndt, screenwriter on *Toy Story 3*, explained his involvement in the project during promotion for the film's theatrical release:

> So they said, 'Hey, Mike, want to write *Toy Story 3*?' I said yes, because they hadn't told me what their ideas were initially. And so it was all the original *Toy Story* creators. John Lasseter, Andrew Stanton, Lee Unkrich, Pete Docter, Bob Peterson, who was a co-director on *Up*, Darla K Anderson, who produced the film, and Jeff Pidgeon, who is an animator, went off to the same original cabin where they came up with the first *Toy Story* idea. The cabin is on the Bay, north of San Francisco. I was told that at the end of the first day they had an idea that they thought was going to work and then they very quickly found out that it wasn't going to work, so then they had nothing. And then they said, 'Well, to get inspired we'll watch the first two *Toy Story* films again.' And they were, like, 'How are we ever going to live up to this?' So it was apparently only on the second day that ideas started to come to them, so that when they went back to me, they had basically had this two day retreat, they got a bunch of ideas, Stanton went off and wrote a 20-page treatment, and in a nutshell basically what they came up with was just this rock solid foundation of the beginning.[163]

In another interview to promote the film, Arndt gave further insight into the intense creative process for *Toy Story 3*, which we might also extrapolate as typical of the studio's other films. 'At Pixar, the script actually gets broken down into 20 or 25 separate sequences. One of them, which we called "Map Hunt" (it's when Woody is in Bonnie's bedroom, trying to figure out how to get home), was written in only six or seven drafts. Most sequences took 20 or 30 drafts. The opening staff meeting, which we called "Grown Up", required 60 drafts.'[164]

And so to the film. We see the Disney logo and there is a cut to a blue sky, and the first image we see is of the iconic, picture–

perfect, abstractly rendered clouds familiar to us from the previous *Toy Story* movies. There is then a cut to the vista of a Pixar-styled American desert, which is to say one whose forms and terrain are more abstracted than those found in *Cars*. The camera dynamically moves in on Mr Potato Head, who is robbing a train. This seems very out of character for the ungainly fellow given his actions in the previous *Toy Story* movies. Indeed, the emphatic quality of the camera move amplifies the effect of the sweeping virtual camera that, many years before, characterised the test footage adapting *Where the Wild Things Are*, which Lasseter and John Musker made at Disney. Sheriff Woody then intervenes in the train robbery, and, in turn, Jessie rescues Woody from certain jeopardy. It's a high-energy sequence that rapidly becomes ever more tense and comic, expanding on the spirit of the previous *Toy Story* chases. More overtly, the sequence connects to the train chase that concludes the brilliantly inventive science-fiction Western, *Back to the Future Part III*. There's something, too, of the kinetic craziness found in the *Road Runner* short films directed by Chuck Jones, and, in this opening sequence, one calamity is superseded by the next even bigger one. We then see that the train that's been hijacked is now filled with orphans. And then, in the next moment, the little green aliens, from *Toy Story* and *Toy Story 2*, turn up alongside the train in a sports car. In this freewheeling sequence, Western icons are being gleefully played around with, making for a thrilling, freely associating riff on the genre. The train then plummets over a cliff edge and Buzz Lightyear comes to the rescue. Indeed, in an instance of 'classic' Pixar foreshadowing, this is effectively a story point that will be echoed at the high-stakes climax of the film.

This prologue, then, is an amazing compendium of toy scenarios. There is then a cut... and we realise that we have been 'inside' Andy's imagination and that he has simply been playing with his toys. It's a self-conscious conceit as smart as that moment when the fridge door opens, thereby concluding the all-animated prelude of *Who Framed Roger Rabbit?* (Robert Zemeckis, 1988). It becomes apparent that Andy has been filmed on home video, and so, as with *Up*, *The Incredibles* and *Toy Story 2*, memory is announced as an important idea in the story. As this prologue concludes, we hear the lyrics of a song playing which includes the phrase 'Our friendship will never die'. The words then fade to a slightly eerie echo, expressing some sense of latent sadness about a way of life fading from view.

There is then a cut to darkness and we realise that we are in the toy chest with the toys. The toys call Andy and he comes in and picks them up. But, significantly, he doesn't play with them, and there's a tinge of sadness on the part of the toys at this moment. It's true to say that the *Toy Story* trilogy is suffused with melancholy, the very same that we find under the roof and the hood of *Up* and *Cars*. One has only to glance at Woody's sad-looking face in this film at the moment when he realises Andy has outgrown the toys. In reaction to this, Woody instigates what he calls Operation Playtime. He makes the point that it's not about being played with; it's about being there for Andy who is going away from home to college. 'Every toy goes through this,' Woody observes, but then, having declared that 'Andy's going to take care of us, I guarantee it,' he looks somewhat uncertain, especially when Buzz replies, rather cynically, 'You guarantee it, huh?'

We see Molly looking into the toy chest and the toys hear Andy's mother talking about how Sunnyside Day Care always needs new playthings. Andy then says the worst thing imaginable, calling the toys 'junk' before putting them in a bin liner. As in *Toy Story* and *Toy Story 2*, the accumulation of minor coincidences builds the drama and jeopardy.

Andy then looks at Woody and Buzz, and the camera is positioned looking up at Andy so that it's his expression that shares the frame with Woody and Buzz in the foreground. The camera then pans to Andy's college box into which he puts Woody only. The other toys are dropped into a black bag and Andy heads for the attic to put them up there. He stops to help Molly and, in that moment, the bag gets picked up by his mother who unthinkingly takes it for trash outside. This scene is a well-realised example of the cause and effect in a mini-narrative and it embodies the idea of chance and fate in the lives of the characters.

Inside the bag the toys immediately try to break free just as the garbage truck arrives. The bags end up in the truck but, in the background, we see that the toys have effectively escaped death.

Nonetheless, the toys face grief at being dumped. They're going through a real emotional ride and, when I first watched the film, I was reminded of the precision with which emotionally stimulating moments can be calibrated in animation. At the Fleischer Studios in New York in the 1920s they originated the Story Mood Chart to show the animation team the 'degree of emotional pace' they were working to on a given project.[165]

The toys then decide to go to Sunnyside and Woody asks Buzz what's going on. He's determined to get everyone back home to the attic: after all, day care is a place for toys without owners. There is then a shot from the toys' point of view as their box gets carried towards the day-care centre. This shot type also occurs in *Toy Story* and *Toy Story 2* and is important in bolstering our connection to the toys – we literally get their view of the world around them as they are taken into the idyllic-looking day-care room.

The Sunnyside toys greet the new arrivals and a purple-coloured, very cuddly looking, friendly sounding teddy bear named Lotso introduces himself. Woody, however, is unconvinced by what Lotso says, particularly when he comments that there's 'no heartbreak' at day care. Woody's scepticism towards Lotso echoes his scepticism towards Buzz in *Toy Story*.

Amongst the toys at Sunnyside are a pair of Ken and Barbie dolls and, as Ken sets about chatting up Barbie, Woody looks dismayed at their fast-flourishing romance.

Sunnyside is very much its own little town and Lotso takes the newly arrived toys into the Caterpillar Room, explaining that this is where they'll live. En route, the toys see a rather spooky doll (Big Baby) with a lazy eye. It evokes the spider toy baby from *Toy Story* and also recalls the menacing baby who makes Tinny's life an anxious one in *Tin Toy*.

The cowgirl Jessie says optimistically that day care could be a whole new life for them all to enjoy but Woody insists they need to be at home for Andy. These toys sure do embody philosophical truths. Contrasting with Woody, Buzz accepts that life now continues at Sunnyside. Is Buzz a pragmatist and Woody an idealist? Buzz says that 'Our mission with Andy is complete now'. Woody's reluctance to accept change makes him a kindred spirit of Bob Parr in *The Incredibles*. Determined to get back to Andy, Woody attempts to escape and there's a very muscular silent comedy quality to the scene in which Woody tries to abscond through the bathroom.

Once on the roof, Woody sees a playground. He manages to get across it and lands in a tree outside the day-care centre where a little girl, Bonnie, picks him up (her rucksack has Wally B on it!).

The action then cuts back to Woody's pals in day care, and suddenly they are invaded as a horde of toddlers runs in, causing chaos as they play. It's a more intensely wrought version of the baby's treatment of Tinny in *Tin Toy*. The action then cuts to Bonnie playing with Woody in her bedroom. Woody talks to the unicorn and Mr Pricklepants and the triceratops. In a fleeting nod to the animated films of Hayao Miyazaki we see a Totoro Plush in Bonnie's room. The action then cuts back to Sunnyside at sundown, the play of light and shade rendered with typical beauty and richness of colour.

As the action unfolds, the rest of the toys think they should be with the older kids in the Butterfly Room. However, the new toys are not as welcome as they initially thought. Buzz watches as Ant, Ken and Rock climb into a snack dispenser. He follows and finds them gambling. Worryingly, he then hears them talking about him. Ant calls them 'toddler fodder'. Buzz is astonished by this discovery and is then found by the creepy baby and immediately put in front of Ken and the other seemingly welcoming toys.

The action then cuts to Woody trying to get home under night skies. As Woody's situation is unresolved the action cuts back to Buzz and his predicament. He is being tied up and Lotso comes to speak to him. Buzz asks to be transferred and Lotso agrees to this. However, Lotso has a Buzz manual and he and his cronies reset

Buzz to stop him proving a threat anymore. Like *A Bug's Life*, *Toy Story 3* is a politically minded film about the oppression of free will and the necessity for identity.

In *Up* and *Monsters, Inc* there were moments of comic lunacy, where the logic of story was trumped by invention. *Toy Story 3* has this, too, and it's in the form of Mrs Potato Head. One of her eyes is still back in Andy's home and so she is able to have a sort of special sight that allows her to see Andy is looking for them all. Immediately, the toys realise that Woody was telling them the truth and that they need to get back to Andy. However, things become complicated when Buzz turns up with his factory-setting behaviour. Lotso looks menacing as he watches Buzz fight. Buzz is 'working' for Lotso now.

Essentially, Buzz is under a spell and so the film is fairy tale-like and certainly the most fairytale-minded chapter in the *Toy Story* saga, and this is in part because of the mournfulness it possesses. The film historian John Canemaker offers us a touching connective tissue here: Joe Ranft, who was vital to Pixar story development and had been involved in developing *Toy Story 3* as well as being vital to many earlier Pixar movies, had died in 2005. Canemaker's assessment of Ranft was this: 'His mentoring of many who are now top Pixar story artists continues to affect the structure and content of the films. I also think the impact of his untimely and tragic death brought Pixar's young artists in general to a sharp, indeed shocking, awareness of life's dark and sad side, the fragility and briefness of our lives, the need to give everything our best shot.'[166] Ranft is memorialised in the film *Coraline*: he is the removal-man character who does not wear a hat.

Barbie then sees Ken and the other toys being mean to Andy's toys. Lotso then explains to Buzz that he will doubt himself (connects to Tow Mater in *Cars 2*).

This theme of self-identity and self-realisation is key to the film and underpins the Pixar philosophical stance. Realising that Bonnie's home is only around the corner from Andy's, Woody's thoughts turn to his toy friends escaping from Sunnyside. Bonnie's toys then explain the darker side of Sunnyside, and this is a surefire example of Pixar's use of memory, both in characters and as a structural device, that we might recognise from *Up* and *Toy Story 2*. Chuckles the Clown explains the Sunnyside story to Woody. Through a charming flashback we learn that Lotso was a little girl's favourite toy. However, the toys were eventually dumped (Lotso, Big Baby and Chuckles) by the roadside. Lotso eventually got back home to Daisy, only to find that she'd replaced him! Lost and alone, the abandoned toys ended up at Sunnyside. The action then cuts from this explanation for Lotso's behaviour to Andy's toys in their cages at Sunnyside.

As Lotso and his cohorts ride in for the start of a new day at Sunnyside, Bonnie also arrives, bringing Woody with her. As Woody climbs out of Bonnie's rucksack, he sees the kids treating the toys terribly.

Woody discovers that each door is locked every night and that there's a toy monkey on security duty who sounds the alarm. This is a nightmarish character, rather like the baby spider in *Toy Story* with its manic demeanour.

Woody is reunited with his pals who explain that Buzz thinks he's a real astronaut again. A race against time now ensues with Woody and the toys needing to get home to Andy before he leaves for college. At this moment, *Toy Story 3* announces its PoW genre credentials. Woody tries to immobilise the monkey, and the toys attempt to escape. Barbie even comes to the rescue by securing the Buzz operating manual so that he can be repaired.

The jeopardy intensifies as Big Baby, now one of Lotso's heavies, nearly finds out that Buzz is attempting to 'reboot' himself and Lotso confronts Woody, asking him with real cruelty, 'If your kid loves you so much, why is he leaving?'

In a moment of redemption, Ken sides with the toys (who function in a very democratic manner) and Woody then mentions Daisy to Lotso. Recalling the unwelcome memory of the past, Lotso grabs Woody and the film's expansive action finale, set around a dump truck and a landfill site, kicks into gear. In a way, the scale of the finale matches the action sequence that began the film. The landfill site has an apocalyptic quality in its lighting and shading. As the scenario unfolds, Lotso becomes stuck and finds himself heading for the jaws of the landfill trash compactor. For all that he has done to make their lives difficult, Woody and Buzz go to help him and Woody says, 'We're all in this together.' Heading for the furnace, Lotso then betrays our heroes who think Lotso is helping them. Finally, the toys roll towards their doom, all holding on to each other. In a narrative device that we can safely refer to as *deus ex machina* the toys are saved from plummeting to their fiery doom by a mechanical claw (in a reversal of the role played by a similar mechanism in *Toy Story*) and then head back home to Andy's bedroom. Woody says goodbye to his pals who are heading for the attic, while Woody gets placed into Andy's college box.

In the film's coda, Andy takes the toys to Bonnie and even gives her Woody so that the toys can continue to live together. This final moment plays out under green trees and blue skies in a fantasia of suburbia.

Given the success of the previous *Toy Story* films, one might expect the third to be under all the more pressure to achieve. Roger Ebert expressed a sense that the film had been a success but not quite on the level of parts one and two: 'This is a jolly, slapstick comedy, lacking the almost eerie humanity that infused the earlier *Toy Story* sagas, and happier with action and jokes than with characters and emotion.'[167]

Not all were effusive. In *Empire* the film was reviewed with the opening question, 'How "adult" can a commercial family movie be pushed before it starts alienating its core audience?'[168]

Elsewhere in this book we've made the connection between *Up* and the Japanese movie *Tokyo Story* and, for all of the kinetic energy of *Toy Story 3*, there are affecting moments of lyricism.

Cars 2 (2011)

Directed by: John Lasseter
Co-directed by: Brad Lewis
Written by: Ben Queen (screenplay), John Lasseter, Brad Lewis and Dan Fogelman (story)
Produced by: Denise Ream
Music by: Michael Giacchino
Edited by: Stephen R Schaffer
Art Direction: Jay Shuster
Production Design: Harley Jessup
Cast: Owen Wilson (Lightning McQueen), Michael Caine (Finn Mc-Missile), Emily Mortimer (Holly)

Just as *Toy Story 3* combined the dynamics of the buddy movie with those of the POW movie, and *The Incredibles* combined action movie with domestic comedy, *Cars 2* is also a genre fusion: part road movie and part spy thriller. It's a movie which pastiches and parodies the spy format.

Ben Queen has explained how 'the nugget of the movie – what the movie is about – the "theme" or whatever you want to call it, seems to inform everything at Pixar. John Lasseter makes sure everyone knows what the character is thinking at a particular moment and what that means to the story overall. And Harley Jessup, Sharon Calahan and others – they make their decisions based on what's best for the emotional throughline of the movie. The colourscript, I think it's called, is a good example of this. I'm sure you're well aware of those. But the decisions about mood, lighting, colour that inform those colourscripts come straight from that nugget. Anyone working on the movie should be able to stand in front of it and go, "Yes, that's how I'm supposed to feel the movie, emotionally."'[169]

Interestingly, *Cars 2* has what we might term an absence of sentiment that makes it appear colder than other Pixar films. Perhaps that is why it was not so highly regarded: it wasn't feelgood in the way that other Pixar movies have tended to be.

The film is a bold demonstration of the studio's facility with story structure as two storylines intertwine and converge: Lightning McQueen competing in a series of races (in Tokyo, Italy and London) whilst a story of corporate greed (oil versus renewable) and deception plays out in the form of a spy thriller.

According to John Lasseter, 'Going back to creating a sequel, you want to find where's the emotion going to come from. You just don't want to revisit the same emotion.'[170]

The film begins with Agent Leland Turbo having his cover compromised as he spies on an immense oil platform 'city'. Leland sends a signal asking for Agent Finn McMissile to come and help him. There follows a brief and visually striking opening credit sequence which establishes the film's action-heavy, spy-movie vibe. The action then centres on a stormy sea at night as a small boat carries Finn McMissile on his mission to aid Leland. The sea has realistic weight and volume and, throughout *Cars 2*, as in all Pixar films, the settings have a photorealistic presence in terms of scale, lighting and texture. They're almost too beautifully realised.

Finn sneaks on to the oil rig and a fast and furious chase ensues as he realises that Leland Turbo has been captured by the bad guys – Professor Zundapp and his henchmen cars. The chase as Finn seeks to escape is rendered with incredible precision of rhythm. As with so many Pixar sequences it's a clear-sighted case study in storytelling technique as it builds tension, then relieves tension, with camera 'placement' communicating the action with maximum clarity. If there's one thing a well-realised popular film does, it's to function as a case study of the clear communication of an idea. The film's Bond-like sensibility is further evoked by the music of Michael Giacchino, which reminds us too of similarly spirited work for *The Incredibles*. Like *Cars 2*, *The Incredibles* parodies a genre known for its typically straight-faced demeanour. The chase has the wit and energy of a Chuck Jones-designed pursuit in a *Road Runner* cartoon and it takes us all the way back to the necessarily brief chase that features in the experimental short that was Pixar's first ever production, *The Adventures of Andre and Wally B*. Like that film, *Cars 2* keeps a firm hold on characterisation amidst the action. Leland gets away and Finn escapes into the depths of the ocean, faking his demise in the process.

The film then cuts from the nighttime, clean lines and hi-tech structures of the oil-rig action sequence and we find ourselves back in the familiar surroundings of the high-key, low-contrast desert environment of Radiator Springs. Once again we meet Tow Mater, the country-boy tow truck, familiar to us from the original *Cars* movie. Lightning's out of town at this point in the story with his racing commitments and Tow Mater is clearly missing him. Tow Mater then becomes aware that Lightning is already back. To bring audiences up to story speed, Mater and Lightning momentarily share their sadness about their mentor Doc Hudson's passing. The pink sunset lends the moment a delicacy and beauty. Pixar knows the emotional notes that colour can strike.

Lightning then explains that he's going to have dinner with Sally and Mater's sad face registers his feelings at not being able to hang out with Lightning.

A news story then breaks which tells of how Miles Axelrod – an oil billionaire – is promoting alternative energy for cars. The World Grand Prix is being hosted by Miles and he invites Lightning to compete. Lightning is grateful but explains that he's having a break from competition. He knows that what's important is to slow down and enjoy life. Tow Mater adds enthusiastically that Lightning is still a great race car.

This sequence of the film then establishes that the Italian car, Francesco, is now Lightning McQueen's main competitor. Unable to resist his competitive instinct Lightning says yes to competing in the race and Sally insists that he must take Mater with him. A brief sequence then follows that charts the journey being made overseas. In Tokyo they see lots of Lightning McQueen toys (it's a moment that might make you think of the wry smile behind the pan across toys at Jurassic Park in *Jurassic Park*). Lightning and Mater arrive for the race and there is a vividly conjured sense of enormity, colour and pageantry. It's a dream of the twenty-first-century megacity that's in total contrast with the rural quiet of Radiator Springs. Lightning takes easily to a foreign land but, for Mater, it's a very different experience. In a moment of narrative foreshadowing of the sort Pixar have always enjoyed utilising, Mater has a scene that will carry more weight later in the film as he watches a Zen gardener at work. This is one of several cultural misunderstandings on Mater's part. Lightning makes the cultural comment that 'things are different over here'. Lightning and his nemesis Francesco meet, the Italian car asserting that 'women respect a car who has nothing to hide'.

Like *Toy Story* and *Monsters, Inc*, *Cars 2* is a buddy movie. Finn McMissile turns up at the Tokyo racetrack and scopes the place. He meets Agent Holly Shiftwell and she explains that the biggest oil reserve in the world has been found. Clearly, there's concern and, at this point, the professor's henchmen turn up. Holly has to stand in for Finn at a rendezvous with the American agent they're due to meet. The action then cuts to a scene in which Mater goes to the bathroom. A case of mistaken identity ensues as Mater is presumed to be the American agent. Mater thinks he's got a date. The scene then cuts to the bad guys hiding out on the Tokyo waterfront whilst the actual American agent Holly was scheduled to meet is imprisoned and held hostage. The sequence then clarifies a key plot point: the TV camera is actually an electromagnetic pulse emitter. The bad guys think that Tow Mater is the second agent and that they are going to kill him. There is then a cut to the first big race. Lightning McQueen's determination and pluck is very boyish and it's partly that which must account for his appeal beyond the movie.

Finn and Holly spy on Tow Mater and mistakenly think that he's the American agent. There is then a shot of the Rainbow Bridge which is very true to sports coverage shots. The bad guys are using the 'camera' to take out cars as they race along. The henchmen see Mater in the pitstop and close in on him. Holly and Finn see this and Holly radios in to say that Tow Mater should get out of the pits. Finn then intercepts the bad guys and a very humorous chase through the Tokyo backstreets ensues which intercuts with the race.

Lightning McQueen selfishly says he doesn't want Tow Mater's help because it's making him looking bad. Tow Mater is rejected again by Lightning. Sure enough, as in *Cars*, Lightning has the experience of hubris and nemesis to learn from.

There is then a cut to Tow Mater alone and sad and the henchmen see him at the airport. Finn, in disguise, gets Tow Mater to follow him. Finn introduces himself as British intelligence. There is then a chase out of the airport, and Finn and Mater board the aeroplane and Mater leaves a goodbye note for Lightning.

Aboard the spy plane Mater soon realises they think that he's a spy. Finn charges Tow Mater with the task of getting information. The action then cuts to Paris where an establishing shot echoes the Parisian settings of *Ratatouille*, particularly in its attention to light playing off surfaces. Safely in Paris, Tow, Finn and Holly try to work out what is going on.

One of the delights of Pixar films is that moment when you can see the gears and chains of a story's structure catching and fluidly moving. Indeed, I'd say that sometimes the narrative mechanics of set-up and pay-off are more compelling to behold than the visuals.

Holly and Finn put Mater into a disguise and, as they do so, try to remove his dents. However, in a philosophical moment, he says that he's proud of his dents so don't get rid of them.

They give Mater his own weapons so that he becomes very much like a souped-up, armoured vehicle that James Bond might drive. He then gets sent into the bad guys' HQ. The action then cuts to Italy where race number two takes place and more cars are being taken out by the 'camera' being deployed by the bad guys. Holly explains that 'they want to get everyone back to using oil as they've got a huge untapped reserve'.

Finn then gets caught en route to getting the guys with the camera gun looking down on the racetrack, and there is then a big pile up in the race because of the bad guys. Holly calls for Mater to leave the villains' HQ as he's in real jeopardy. At the racetrack the order is given for Lightning McQueen to be killed and Mater's cover is blown. There is a big shoot out from which Mater just about escapes. Tow then goes to rescue Lightning and Mater shouts out to Lightning, 'They're going to kill you.'

Mater is then captured by the bad guys and, in a moment of quiet in a very busy film, there's a connection with the form of the *Toy Story* movies, *The Incredibles* and *Up* as the power of memory comes to the rescue of the hero and Mater remembers all the instances when he's been laughed at. The clown who becomes more serious is rather like the young man who is the butt of others' jokes and who eventually succeeds in folk tales.

In London, Mater, Finn and Holly have been imprisoned inside Big Bentley. 'You were right, Finn, I'm a fool,' Mater says, hitting his low point at the moment when he needs to be ready for action. The villains' henchmen then turn up and they're going to kill Lightning. As the situation deteriorates the skies of London become increasingly grey and ominous. When the bad guys target McQueen's engine with their camera gun nothing happens. Tow Mater's sense of self appears to have fallen apart and he explains to Holly that 'I'm just a tow truck'. Holly then connects with Tow's pride in his life and says, 'Go and get some more dents, Mater.' Renewed, rather like Carl is renewed for adventure just in time, Mater goes to rescue Lightning and Finn and Holly escape. The stakes then mount when we realise that the bomb is actually a Tow Mater. Order is restored and Tow learns to be himself. Miles is actually revealed as the bad guy and Tow Mater gets knighted.

The action then cuts back to Radiator Springs where we see Tow telling his stories. Even Finn and Holly arrive.

Cars 2 was hugely popular commercially but was regarded as less creatively successful than previous Pixar movies. I don't know if this is quite the case. It certainly doesn't have the sentimentality of other Pixar films and so perhaps this absence is what surprised reviewers. However, as smart and genre-savvy parody and pastiche it works brilliantly; it's got something of the self-conscious smarts of a film like *Back to the Future, Part II* (Robert Zemeckis, 1989).

Patrick Goldstein, writing about Pixar in the context of *Cars 2*, commented in a piece entitled 'Is Pixar's Winning Streak Over?' that

'Pixar won't have much luck starting a new streak if its fearless leader continues to be in denial about the fact that he whiffed this last time out, artistically speaking. What made Pixar great was its ability to be self critical. But the system broke down with *Cars 2*. Was Lasseter too distracted running Pixar when he should have been focused on filmmaking? Did Disney's corporate push to turn films into brands overwhelm Pixar's quality control system?'[171]

Cars 2 did not receive an Academy Award nomination and this was a new experience for Pixar, who had won the Best Animated Feature award four years in a row. However, the film was the most commercially popular animated film of the year. As a whole, Pixar's films until 2011 had grossed $6.5 billion globally.

Roger Ebert enthused about the film, saying that it was 'an international racing and spying thriller as wacky as a Bond picture crossed with Daffy Duck'.[172] *Empire* magazine was a little more reserved and considered the film 'not vintage Pixar'.[173]

Brave (2012)

Directed by: Brenda Chapman and Mark Andrews
Written by: Brenda Chapman, Mark Andrews, Steve Purcell, Irene Mecchi (screenplay), Brenda Chapman (story)
Produced by: Katherine Sarafian
Music by: Patrick Doyle
Sound by: EJ Holowicki
Edited by: Nicholas C Smith
Production Design: Paul Abadilla
Cast: Kelly Macdonald (Merida), Emma Thompson (Elinor), Billy Connolly (Fergus), Julie Walters (The Witch), Robbie Coltrane (Lord Dingwall)

In early March of 2012 a Japanese teaser poster for *Brave* was released along with a trailer fashioned for the Japanese audience. This teaser poster was arrestingly different to the one released in America in that it emphasised the lyrical and the numinous. Critically, the humour of the film was not foregrounded but instead its sense of mystery and the numinous were the qualities that mattered most in this campaign. Certainly, the poster image evoked a feeling we might identify from the Studio Ghibli film *Princess Mononoke* (1997) with its expression of a pantheistic spirit that has proved so compelling and attractive to audiences around the globe. Indeed, the film's connection to 'ancient' tradition, and a moment in time, has been its defining marketing characteristic for Japan where such ideas remain strong and which, certainly, in terms of Hayao Miyazaki films, are key to the films that he directs.

Brenda Chapman, who originally conceived the film, originally entitled *The Bear and the Bow*, started out as its sole director. Chapman is notable for having been the first woman to direct a major Hollywood studio animated feature with the elegantly rendered cel animated movie *The Prince of Egypt* (1998). Since then, Jennifer Yuh Nelson has directed *Kung Fu Panda 2* (2011). Alas, Chapman eventually stepped away from the film before its release on account of creative differences. In developing *Brave*, Chapman sought to anchor the more fantastical elements of the story in a recognisable and resonant relationship dynamic between a mother and her growing daughter.

In 2011, Chapman made the following observation: 'I think it's a really sad state. We're in the 21st century and there are so few stories geared towards girls, told from a female point of view.'[174]

In the buildup to *Brave* (Pixar enthusiasts had been anticipating it for two or three years) the film was much talked about as the first Pixar movie with a female protagonist. For commercial imperatives the film was retitled *Brave* in an effort to broaden its appeal. A similar choice had been made in retitling Disney's *Rapunzel* to *Tangled*.

The third *Brave* trailer, released in April 2012, emphasised in parts the film's focus on Merida's search for a new sense of self and this aspect of the story was key to its interest. Ahead of the film's theatrical release *Time* magazine ran an article on 5 March 2012 entitled 'Pixar's Girl Story'. The author of the piece was Joel Stein and he made the observation that 'Pixar has a girl problem. All twelve of its unfathomably successful movies [...] have male leads.'

Certainly the film excels in the performances that it offers, especially in terms of a bear character that is central to the story. As such, film showcases a point that Ed Hooks has made in his comment that 'animators have to pitch camp at the intersection of movement and emotion'. At key points the emotion of the bear, despite its great size, is expressed most powerfully through the detail of animation of the eyes and eyebrows.

In *Brave*, Merida desperately wants to subvert the expectation of how a girl should be in the world. Merida wants to move beyond the demands and constrictions of home and explore the wider world. As such, she is something of a soulmate to Remy in *Ratatouille* and Carl in *Up*. All three characters are emblems of the questing curiosity that we hope makes for a satisfying life.

NEW PIXAR FEATURE FILMS

Monsters University

In the summer of 2013, Pixar released the sequel to *Monsters, Inc.* The story was in fact set before the events of the original film, exploring how Mike and Sulley met as students. Styled in the mode of a frat-house comedy the film was described by *Slate* magazine as follows: 'This time around, we learn that being a "scarer" is one of the most prestigious and desirable jobs in the monster world, which makes *Monsters University*, amongst other things, a film about the anxieties of meritocracy.'[175]

The Good Dinosaur

In early August 2013, at the D23 (Disney's convention for its fan club members) and after much anticipation, Pixar was able to screen initial footage from *The Good Dinosaur* (which is due to be released in late 2014) and also show production artwork. Even the title is redolent of a children's picture book of many years' standing. The film's premise focuses on the fact that dinosaurs did not become extinct but instead walked amongst the first humans. The dinosaur, an Apatosaurus named Arlo, befriends a child named Spot. Twenty years ago, with Steven Spielberg's classic *Jurassic Park*, the beasts, always popular, enjoyed a real resurgence that's sustained itself ever since. Indeed, Spielberg also produced *We're Back!*, released in autumn 1993 but relatively little seen. An animated movie, it adapts Hudson Talbott's book of the same name and concerns itself with dinosaurs in modern New York. For young children the enormity of a dinosaur might suggest either terror or a sense of protection and, visually, as *The Good Dinosaur*'s production art has already shown, there is much humour to be enjoyed in the differences in size.

So far, John Lasseter has been willing to say this about the film's protagonists: 'They are kind of cartoony but they are dinosaurs; they are not walking around with clothes on or anything like that, they still are kind of dinosaurs. We focused on mostly the plant-eaters, not the carnivores [...] Their society becomes more of an agrarian society, meaning farmers. They become farmers. It's a very funny story about a certain way of life that a young dinosaur has trouble fitting into and he ends up going on this quest. He kind of messes up and has to put everything right by going on this quest and, on that quest, he meets a character that is an outcast from his society too, and so the two of them form this bond and it becomes this unique kind of story.'[176]

Inside Out

The fundamental idea for this forthcoming movie might make you think of the Disney animated short from World War Two entitled *Reason and Emotion*. *Inside Out* is written and directed by Pete Docter and, like his two previous Pixar movies, *Monsters, Inc* and *Up*, there's a very playful quality to the premise. Alongside *Ratatouille* it might be the studio's most nicely bizarre-sounding concept to date. The film's protagonist is an eleven-year-old girl named Riley and the film explores the relationship between Riley and the emotions that dominate her brain (her reason?). Joy, Anger, Disgust, Sadness and Fear are entities that Riley must deal with and the film also appears to relish the chance to visualise, in very literal ways, typically abstract phrases and terms that we are familiar with in terms of how our minds function. Hence, the preview of the film at D23 included an image of an actual Train of Thought. The character designs include typically expressive faces in which the eyes do so much to communicate emotion and thought. Abstract Thought resembles a Picasso painting for example.

Finding Dory

Returning to animated moviemaking after his hugely entertaining fantasy adventure movie *John Carter* (2012), Andrew Stanton has written and is directing the sequel to *Finding Nemo*. In this story, Dory is searching for her family with Marlin and Nemo assisting on the quest.

Day of the Dead Film

Certainly, Tim Burton's *The Nightmare Before Christmas*, the computer game *Grim Fandango* and, much more recently, DreamWorks Animation's *Rise of the Guardians* have creatively interpreted the visual opportunities present in a number of autumn- and winter-themed festivals and national holidays. Lee Unkrich's film suggests something more blackly comic than Pixar films have typically tended to be.

PIXAR'S SHORT FILMS

Some years ago now I was running a series of filmmaking workshops. I booked a director with a proven track record in short film projects for the BBC's long-lost *10 x 10* series and, as he stood before his class, he did, I think, startle them when he explained that Pixar's films were amongst the best to watch in order to get a valuable understanding of film screenplay structure, characterisation and so forth. The short-film format offers an even more concentrated example of these 'lessons'.

Sometimes the best way to gauge what a film is capable of and how dynamic it can be is to watch a short film. Just consider *The Red Balloon*, *Neighbours*, and any *Tom and Jerry* cartoon. The concision of the form tends to encourage the filmmaker to particular invention and certainly to move away from any kind of emphasis on speech; instead, speech is de-emphasised.

Well, what's a short film for? In the most pragmatic terms, it's a good testing ground for emerging filmmakers and also the application of new technologies. In terms of story it's a wonderful means of concise expression and tends to work best when it's not a feature film condensed. Watching animated short films is one of the best filmmaking educations you can get in terms of storytelling rules being enforced and broken.

Pixar's short films apply much humour and invention and work very well as concentrated fairy tale and folk tale forms. The Pixar films in part serve to allow the studio to explore new technologies and have also provided opportunities for directors to make their mark and from there perhaps move into feature-film animation directing.

The Adventures of Andre and Wally B

The pastel illustration of Andre B by John Lasseter is identifiable as a Pixar character in its proportions, its expressive eyes.

In 1984, Pixar (still at Lucasfilm then) had produced a short that ran under two minutes called *The Adventures of Andre and Wally B* about a bee who gives a fellow a hard time as he tries to take it easy in a blissfully sunny forest, the brightness of which anticipates the look of *A Bug's Life*. Significant in this film was the creation of motion blur, that is to say the lack of definition that moving objects have as they pass through a space. Short though the film is, it took months of computer power to process using, as had been done on *The Last Starfighter*, the Cray computer systems.

The film starts with a wideshot of a nature scene that somewhat anticipates the beautiful rendering of nature in the films *A Bug's Life* and *Up*. The camera pans down from a vista showing the sun rising over the top of a hill. It then comes to rest on a glade where a figure is lying down. He sits up. This is Andre. A bee (Wally B) then buzzes into frame and approaches Andre, nose to nose with him virtually. Andre flees from Wally who pursues, and a series of shots charts the chase with great energy and dynamism.

Luxo Jr

Luxo Jr is another simple and hugely engaging 'experimental' film that Pixar made in its earliest moment. Of the project, John Lasseter has made the point that 'one of the things I always do with inanimate objects – to make an object look like it's thinking the first thing you do is identify its face and its head. Being a light I sort of thought with the light coming out that's the vision, the head.'

Red's Dream

Red's Dream is a charming short that focuses on a unicycle who dreams of a better place to be.

Tin Toy

Tin Toy was a project prompted by an idea suggested to John Lasseter when watching a home video showing his son repeatedly slamming a toy up and down. 'If I was a toy, that [child] would be a horrible monster,' Lasseter has explained. Certainly, *Tin Toy* is one of the most significant early Pixar films and it was the first to use Renderman software for the animation of a human character (the baby).

The film tells the story of Tinny, a one-man-band toy, who, seeing a baby crying, sets out to make him smile again. In doing so, Tinny is terrified by the immense-looking baby who chases him all over the room. Tinny even finds other toys cowering in terror beneath a sofa. For the *Tin Toy* short, Tinny had to have 40 facial muscles virtually created in the computer. Although he never speaks, Tinny clearly registers happiness, terror and sadness. The film begins with the camera panning over the floor and it moves past an opened tin-toy box, the completely fabricated digital image selling us on the illusion of cardboard packaging. The camera then booms down to offer a medium-close-up shot on Tinny, the tin toy soldier at the centre of the story. It's a fluid camera move that recalls the work on display in Lasseter and Keane's 1983 test footage for *Where the Wild Things Are*.

Tinny looks cautiously around, his eyes (again, the eyes are so very much the window of the soul in animation) communicating everything they are thinking and feeling. Every time Tinny blinks there is a rather cute mechanical clinking sound to accompany this very ordinary physical action. Tinny's reflective surface believably looks metallic and, to anyone watching the film having first viewed *Toy Story*, they'll easily recognise the influence of the design of Tinny and also the larger narrative connection between both films. How interesting to think what audiences would have made of *Toy Story* in 1995 if they had been familiar with *Tin Toy* from seven years previously.

As with *The Adventures of Andre and Wally B*, *Tin Toy* is a chase story. There's even a sense of mounting jeopardy as Tinny, in trying to flee the baby, gets himself trapped in the box from which he came. Tinny then hides beneath the sofa only to find a number of other toys looking back at him who have also taken refuge. This is the moment that's most redolent, or anticipatory, of *Toy Story*. The film's use of sound is critical, the squeezebox that Tinny has between 'his' hands sounding forlorn or agitated depending on his circumstances. Tinny then emerges from below the sofa and plays his cymbals for the baby who is a little distressed. The baby then picks Tinny up and shakes him wildly like King Kong holding Fay Wray.

Tin Toy was the first computer-animated short to win an Oscar, building on the success of *Luxo Jr* (1986).

Intriguingly, the original concept for *Toy Story* starred Tinny, who gets lost and befriends a ventriloquist's dummy, and together they hit the road and end up in a safe haven – a preschool where they can never get lost. Indeed, Tinny, the hero of *Tin Toy*, was initially going to be a central character in *Toy Story* until Buzz Lightyear was dreamt up. Amusingly, in retrospect, the Pixar software in 1986 was referred to as 'a rich kid's toy' by the former General Manager of ILM, Thomas G Smith, in his immense book *Industrial Light and Magic: The Art of Special Effects*.[177]

Knick Knack

Knick Knack builds on *Tin Toy*'s humour, being a story that essentially tells the Myth of Sisyphus in which a man rolls a boulder to the top of a hill only to watch it roll back down. Very much in the spirit of a *Road Runner* cartoon, with the snowman knick knack being the equivalent to Wile E Coyote, the film simply relates the attempts of the knick knack to break out of its glass ball and go and party with the knick knacks across from him on the shelf. He's especially attracted to the curvaceous girl knick knack. The film's timing is exquisite, comedy and tragedy as one and with a final sight gag that *Jurassic Park* uses.

Geri's Game

This short film was the first to centre on a human protagonist, focusing on two sides of one elderly man's personality as he plays chess. The setting of the short emphasises the rather beautiful colours of an autumn day. Geri is sufficiently caricatured but is photorealistically lit and shaded. The film applies effective editing pace to enhance the conflicting personalities and, in a way, it's Pixar's first not-so-sweet short film.

For the Birds

Another of Pixar's *Aesop's Fables*, in spirit at least. We see a remote rural spot and a telegraph line on to which drop numerous plump and cute little birds. They chirp and chatter and then hear a rather goofy sounding squawk and see a much larger bird who comes to rest precariously on the line. The birds don't want the outsider there and so peck him off the line. The big bird has the last laugh and the birds pay the price for not welcoming a different bird with open wings. The moment when each of the big bird's toes slips from the wire has the comic timing of a Chuck Jones *Road Runner* short when a character recognises things are about to go very wrong.

One Man Band

Just as Woody and Buzz in the *Toy Story* films endlessly bicker and try to outdo each other in their fits of jealousy and envy, so too do the two musicians in this film. They compete for the one gold coin of a little girl in a medieval-era European market square. The film is an exercise in comic timing with no recourse to the use of dialogue. The little girl's face registers forlornness and then anger and, as with *Geri's Game*, editing is used to build a frenzied pace as egos (and, therefore, emotion) are the source of the film's intrigue.

Boundin'

Nothing less than a confidently styled American tall tale that maybe evokes the spirit of Mark Twain, *Boundin'* uses a charming song to narrate, in part, the story of a sheep who loses its sense of value when shorn of its wool. It takes a happy, optimistic jackrabbit to help the pensive sheep look at life afresh.

Presto

Showcasing confidently realised comic pacing, *Presto* tells the story of a magician and its rabbit. Gesture, facial expression and dynamic use of sound effects communicate all that we need to know. It also features a very cute looking and sounding rabbit whose only interest is in the carrot it wants to eat rather than a successful magic show. The laws of physics, space and time all get thoroughly lampooned in this smart silent film about professional pride coming before plenty of falls. It's certainly got something of the sensibility of a *Road Runner* cartoon about it.

Partly Cloudy

We immediately think of *Dumbo*, perhaps, as storks fly in over suburbia to deliver newborn pets. We follow a stork back up into the sky where babies are being made by the clouds. The clouds are happy and pink with one exception: a forlorn-faced, grey cloud who only seems able to make less than cute animals: crocodiles, hedgehogs. The ever faithful stork carries out his work and then flies to another cloud. The grey cloud looks very sad but the stork returns, this time wearing a football helmet and pads for protection, able to deliver whatever the grey cloud makes. It's all about adapting to circumstances, enjoying one's own self, and not being like the others.

Day and Night

Has the feel of a 1950s cartoon. Two abstract forms, though with arms, legs and faces, move across a black background. Within each form we see day and night, the pleasures of each playing out. Day and Night compete with each other to state that their time of the day or night is best. Eventually, they find that they can only exist together.

La Luna

In discussing his short film *La Luna*, director Enrico Casarosa described the development process for the short, which speaks as well of the feature-making process, when he explained that 'John

(Lasseter) and his team like to see three ideas – so I worked for maybe three months preparing three pitches... The first time I pitched, I pitched it with image boards, beat boards. I made 20-something watercolours. So after the go-ahead, the next step was to board it. And slowly, you're aiming for locking your storyboards, creating your story reel. Once you're locked for that, you can really start production.'[178]

The Blue Umbrella

One of the pleasures that Pixar movies include is space for lyricism; for a pause amidst the typically high energy dynamic of their films. *The Blue Umbrella* is a short that was initially attached to *Monsters University*. Taking the Pixar modus operandi of making the familiar fresh and unfamiliar this film is a love story in which the simplest of facial expressions are to be seen on a blue (boy) and red (girl) umbrella. Again reminding us of the power of the silent film, this animated short is elegant, lyrical and very moving.

Currently, more *Toy Story* toons (shorts) and *Cars* shorts are in the works, as well as a new series of shorts entitled *Planes*.

POSTSCRIPT

We might say that our lives are stories and so any film that can draw out this quality affixes itself to our thoughts, our feelings, our memories, our understandings. It's in animated film that we so often see this magic worked. Speaking about the related form of comics, Jack Kirby, the legendary American comic artist, made a comment that serves as just the right coda to *The Incredibles*. Kirby described comics as 'a democratic art'. Surely this, too, is true of the animated movie.

Animated films, with their strong ties to illustration from the most ancient, deep history until today, have the capacity to be entirely the product of human imagination and truly become talismans that stay with us, keeping us young, keeping our view of the world alive and animated in a way that takes us right back to the beginning and the root meaning of the word: animus. When I was growing up, first in southwest London and then in a rural market town, my way into the wider world was very much provided by movies. Movies gave that extra lift to the view and so I hope that, in its modest way, this book communicates that fascination with movies.

It feels only right to conclude this book with a tip of the hat to the late, great Arthur Rackham. Long ago, this genius of an illustrator, whose work was synonymous with plenty of fantasy stories, summed up the spirit of his work by saying that 'Like the sundial, my paintbox counts no hours but sunny ones.'

ENDNOTES

1   Brad Bird, http://animationartconservation.com/?c=art&p=articles-ratatouille
2   Brian Boyd, *The Origin of Stories*, Belknap Press of Harvard University Press, 2009, p.2
3   Norman Klein, *7 Minutes: The Life and Death of the American Cartoon*, Verso Books, 1995, p.23
4   Jack Zipes, *The Oxford Companion to Fairy Tales*, Oxford University Press, 2002, p.xviii
5   Randy Thom, interviewed by Jane Ganahl, With an ear for storytelling, Randy Thom makes audiences believe what they hear, www.sfgate.com/entertainment/article/with-an-ear-for-storytelling-Randy-Thom-makes-2697099.php
6   *Bantha Tracks*, issue 26, Autumn 1984, published by Lucasfilm
7   *The Oxford Companion to United States History*, Oxford University Press, 2001, p.674
8   Joseph Campbell, *The Flight of the Wild Gander*, New World Library, 2002, p.76
9   Thomas Hoving, *The Great Art Communicator in Norman Rockwell: Pictures For the American People*, Abrams, 1999
10   Pixar Press release promoting release of new Renderman software, www.cartoonbrew.com
11   Paul Auster, NY Library podcast
12   Steve Jobs, Lucasfilm/Pixar press release, 3 February 1986 - Cartoonbrew.com
13   Ed Catmull, Lucasfilm/Pixar press release, 3 February 1986 - Cartoonbrew.com, 23 February 2011
14   Roger Smith writing about Pixar and Steve Jobs in *With Pixar, Steve Jobs built a paradise for creativity that became a money machine*, Film Comment, 2012 http://www.filmcomment.com/article/passion-project-steve-jobs-built-a-paradise
15   Ed Catmull in Cinefex, *Studio Profile*: Pixar, no.55, August 1993, p.23
16   Michael Barrier in *Huffington Post*, www.cartoonbrew.com, 25 February 2011
17   John Lasseter, *Guardian*, 12 February 2009, www.guardian.co.uk/technology/2009/feb/12/interview-john-lasseter-pixar
18   Norman Klein, *7 Minutes: The Life and Death of the American Cartoon*, Verso Books, 1993, p.26
19   Brian Boyd, *On the Origin of Stories: Evolution, Cognition and Fiction*, Belknap Press of Harvard University Press, 2009, p.360
20   Paul Wells quoted by James Clarke, *State of the Animation Nation*, *Moviescope* magazine, Issue 35, July/August 2013, p.25

21 Norman Klein, *7 Minutes: The Life and Death of the American Cartoon*, Verso Books, 1993, p.204

22 Benjamin Franklin quotation, http://www.quotationspage.com/quote/34348.html

23 Arthur C Clarke, http://www.brainyquote.com/quotes/quotes/a/arthurccl101182.html

24 Sergei Eisenstein quoted by Esther Leslie in *Hollywood Flatlands: Animation, Critical Theory and the Avant-Garde*, Verso Books, 2004, p.230

25 Goethe quoted by Esther Leslie in *Hollywood Flatlands: Animation, Critical Theory and the Avant-Garde*, Verso Books, 2004, p.264

26 Maureen Furniss, *Art in Motion: Animation Aesthetics*, 2008, John Libbey Books, p.67

27 Andrew Sarris on authorship – see 24 June 2012 davidbordwell.net www.davidbordwell.net/articles/Bordwell_Wide%20Angle_vol16_no1_4.pdf

28 David Bordwell in bordwell.net, *A Glimpse Into the Pixar Kitchen*, http://www.davidbordwell.net/blog/2008/04/10/a-glimpse-into-the-pixar-kitchen/

29 Michael Barrier, review of Neal Gabler biography of Walt Disney: http://www.michaelbarrier.com/Commentary/Gabler/GablerBook.htm

30 Jack Zipes, *The Oxford Companion to Fairy Tales*, Oxford University Press, 2002, p.xvii

31 Norman Klein, *7 Minutes: The Life and Death of the Cartoon*, Verso Books, 1993, p.3

32 Hans Christian Andersen, www.brainyquote.com/quotes/quotes/h/hansschrift192605.html

33 Michael Chabon, *Kids Stuff in Maps and Legends: Reading and Writing Along the Borderlands*, McSweeney's Books, 2008, p.87

34 John Lasseter and Hayao Miyazaki, cartoonbrew, 29 July 2009, www.cartoonbrew.com/anime/haya-miyazakijohn-lasseter-press-conference-15440.html

35 Hayao Miyazaki – www.midnighteye.com/interviews/hayaomiyazaki

36 Linda S Watts, *Introduction to The Encyclopedia of American Folklore*, Checkmark Books, 2007, p.viii

37 Ibid, p.ix

38 Scott Cutler Shershow, *Puppets and Popular Culture*, Cornell University Press, 1995, p.2

39 Ibid

40 Brad Bird, interview with Michael Barrier www.michaelbarrier.com/Interviews/Bird/Bird_interview.html

41 Alison Lurie, *Boys and Girls Forever*, Vintage Books, 2004 p.4

42 Carol Stabile and Mark Harrison, *Prime Time Animation: Television Animation and American Culture*, Routledge, 2003, p.1

43 Ibid

44 Cartoonbrew – *Pixar is Silly Symphonies?* www.cartoonbrew.com/disney/if-disney-is-mickey-mouse-is-pixasr-silly-symphonies-8946.html

45 Cartoonbrew.com/cgi/dreamworks-will-release-23-features-through-spring-2016.html

46 *Time Out* – 'Pixar versus Ghibli' www.timeout.com/london/feature/1307/ghibli-vs-pixar-an-animated-debate

47 Ed Catmull, http://hbr.org/2008/09/how-pixar-fosters-collective-creativity/ar/1

48 Brian Boyd, *The Origin of Stories: Evolution, Cognition and Fiction*, The Belknap Press of Harvard University Press, 2009, p.232

49 Kido Shiro quoted by Donald Richie in *A Hundred Years of Japanese Film*, Kodansha International, 2005, chapter 2

50 Bruno Bettelheim, *The Uses of Enchantment: The Meaning and Importance of Fairy Tales*, Penguin Books, 1991

51 Ellen Wolff, *Firms Plan CGI Pix for Infinity and Beyond*, article in *Variety*, 23 March 1997, http://variety.com/1997/scene/vpage/firm-plans-cgi-pix-for-infinity-and-beyond-1117342394/

52 Marina Warner, Animals in Fairytales, *Guardian*, 16 October 2009, www.theguardian.com/2009/oct/16/beastly-tales-warner?wbtrack:NGZiMDk30GEtNDJmOTQOYTY=

53 Kristine Brunovska Karnick and Henry Jenkins, *Classical Hollywood Comedy*, AFI Film Readers, Routledge, 1995, p.2

54 Ibid

55 http://www.kinema.uwaterloo.ca/article.php?id=141

56 Richard Thompson, *Meep Meep*, in *Movies and Methods*, vol 1, edited by Bill Nichols, University of California Press, 1976, p.128

57 L Frank Baum, quoted by James Clarke in *The Virgin Film Guide: Animated Films*, Virgin Books, 2004, p.18

58 Ed Hooks, *Acting for Animators: A Complete Guide to Performance Animation*, Heinemann, 2003, p.19

59 Manohla Dargis, *Summer Movies: Defending Goliath*, New York Times, http://www.nytimes.com/2007/05/06/movies/moviesspecial/06darg.html?_r=0

60 Jack Zipes, www.salon.com/2011/08/20/fairy_tale_movies

61 Alison Lurie, *Boys and Girls Forever*, Vintage Books, 2004, p.2

62 Estelle Shay, *Company Profile: Pixar*, Cinefex, August 1993, no.55, p.23

63 Ibid

64 Eric Smoodin, *Disney Discourse: Producing the Magic Kingdom*, AFI Film Readers, edited by Eric Smoodin, Routledge, 1994, p.6

65 John Lasseter quoted by Rita Street, *Toys Will Be Toys*, Cinefex, December 1995, p.80

66 Richard Edlund, ASC podcast on *Poltergeist*, http://podbay.fm/show/259748235/e/1230755476

67 Ralph Guggenheim quoted by Estelle Shay, *Company Profile: Pixar*, Cinefex no. 55, August 1993, p.24

68 Interview with Ken Schretzmann, from *Moviemaker* magazine, www.moviemaker.com/editing/page2/pixar_editing_ken_schretzmann_20110706

69 John Lasseter quoted by Rita Street, *Toys Will Be Toys*, Cinefex 64, December 1995, p.83

70 Ibid

71 Tom Hanks on comedy in *Film Comment*, www.filmcomment.com/article/a-blast-from-the-past-interview-with-tom-hanks

72 Tim Allen, interview about *Toy Story 3*, http://www.gonewiththetwins.com/pages/interviews/2010/interview_toystory3.php

73 Ralph Eggleston quoted by Rita Street, *Toys Will Be Toys*, *Cinefex* 64, December 1995, p.83

74 *Time Out* review of *Toy Story*, http://www.timeout.com/london/film/toy-story-1995

75 Glenn McNatt, *Re-Examining Rockwell* , Baltimore Sun, 19 June 2000, http://articles.baltimoresun.com/2000-06-19/features/0006190015_1_norman-rockwell-rockwell-illustrated-paintings

76 George Lucas on Rockwell, http://www.cbsnews.com/2300-207_162-10003992-2.html

77 Mary Ann Skweres, *Music For Animation: The Golden Years*, http://www.awn.com/interstitial/interstitial.php?referer=http%3A//www.awn.com/articles/music-animation-golden-years

78 *Box Office* magazine review quoted by James Clarke in *Virgin Film Guide: Animated Film*, 2004

79 Kenneth Turan review of *Toy Story* in *LA Times*, 22 November 1995

80 *Time Out*, http://www.timeout.com/london/film/toy-story-1995

81 *Guardian*, http://www.theguardian.com/film/2009/oct/01/toy-story-3d-review

82 Mark Twain, *Mark Twain's Autobiography*, http://www.twainquotes.com/Heroes.html

83 Jonathan Romney, *Sight and Sound*, 8.12, December 1998, pp.41–42

84 Laura Gibbs – Introduction to *Aesop's Fables*, Oxford World Classics, Oxford University Press, 2008, p.xi

85 Walter Benjamin quoted by Esther Leslie in *Hollywood Flatlands*, Verso Books, 2004, p.83

86 John Lasseter quoted by Mark Cotta Vaz, *A Bug's Life: An Entomological Epic*, *Cinefex* 76, January 1999

87 Maureen Furniss, *Art in Motion: Animation Aesthetics*, Revised Edition, John Libbey Press, 2008, p.20

88 Chris Barker, *Cultural Studies: Theory and Practice*, Third Edition, Sage, London, 2008, p.52

89 Roger Ebert, review of *A Bug's Life*, 25 November 1998, http://www.rogerebert.com/reviews/a-bugs-life-1998

90 *Sight and Sound* review of *A Bug's Life*, http://old.bfi.org.uk/sightandsound/review/26

91 *Time Out* review of *A Bug's Life*, http://www.timeout.com/london/film/a-bugs-life

92 David Bordwell, *Live with it! There'll always be more sequels. Good thing, too*, 20 May 2007, http://www.davidbordwell.net/blog/2007/05/20/live-with-it-therell-always-be-movie-sequels-good-thing-too/

93   John Lasseter quoted by Estelle Shay, *Beyond Andy's Room, Cinefex* 81, April 2000

94   Ibid

95   Richard Dyer, *Entertainment and Utopia, Movies and Methods*, University of California Press, 1985, vol. 2, p.222

96   Ed Hooks, *Acting For Animators: A Complete Guide to Performance*, Routledge, 2011, p.90

97   Ibid

98   Roger Ebert, review of *Toy Story 2*, 24 November 1999, http://www.rogerebert. com/reviews/toy-story-2-1999

99   SFGate.com review of *Toy Story 2*, http://www.sfgate.com/movies/article/ Toy-Story-2-Plays-It-by-Heart-Splendid-sequel-2732900.php

100   *Sight and Sound* review of *Toy Story 2*, http://old.bfi.org.uk/sightandsound/ review/566

101   Marina Warner, *Managing Monsters: Six Myths of our Time*, Vintage UK, 1994, www.marinawarner.com/publications/bookdetailsnonfiction/managingmonsters. html

102   Jim Henson, http://www.goodreads.com/author/quotes/4427.Jim_Henson

103   Bruno Bettelheim, *The Uses of Enchantment: The Meaning and Importance of Fairy Tales*, 1976

104   John Goodman interviewed by Paul Fischer, http://www.crankycritic.com/qa/ pf_articles/johngoodman.html

105   Pete Docter, http://www.pixartalk.com/feature-films/monsters-inc/monsters- inc-production-notes/

106   Marina Warner, *No Go, The Bogeyman*, Chatto and Windus, 1998, p.144

107   Norman Klein, *7 Minutes: The Life and Death of the American Cartoon*, Verso Books, 1996, p.1

108   Peter Bradshaw, review of *Monsters, Inc* in the *Guardian*, http://www. theguardian.com/film/2002/feb/08/1

109   *Sight and Sound* review of *Monsters, Inc*, http://old.bfi.org.uk/sightandsound/ issue/200202

110   Roger Ebert review of *Monsters, Inc.*, http://www.rogerebert.com/reviews/ monsters-inc-2001

111   Andrew Stanton, www.cgsociety.org/index.php/CGSFeatures/CGSFeatures Special/the-making-of-finding-nemo

112   John Lasseter, ibid

113   Ralph Eggleston, ibid

114   Dylan Brown, ibid

115   Thomas Newman, www.editorsguild.com/v2/magazine/Newsletter/newman. html

116   Brad Bird, *Welcome to Planet Pixar* in *Wired*, Issue 12.06, June 2004

117   Brad Bird, www.awn.com/articles/people/nancy-cartwright-chats-brad-bird/ page/3%2CI

118 Michael Tueth on *The Simpsons*, *Prime Time Animation: Television Animation and American Culture*, edited by Carol A Stabile and Mark Harrison, Routledge, 2003, p.139

119 Brad Bird interviewed by Michael Barrier, http://www.michaelbarrier.com/Interviews/Bird/Bird_Interview.htm

120 Maureen Furniss, *Art in Motion: Animation Aesthetics*, John Libbey Books, Revised Edition, 2008, p.6

121 Michael Giacchino interviewed by *Soundtrack.Net*, http://www.soundtrack.net/content/article/?id=132

122 *Slant – A Pixar Week Compendium – Focus on the Family: Pixar's Small-c Conservatism* www.slantmagazine.com/house/2009/10/focus-on-the-family-pixars-smallc-convervatism

123 Roger Ebert, review of *The Incredibles*, http://www.rogerebert.com/reviews/the-incredibles-2004

124 *Guardian*, http://www.guardian.co.uk/film/movie/102423/incredibles

125 *New York Times*, http://movies.nytimes.com/movie/287450/The-Incredibles/overview

126 Gary Gorth interview with Jack Kirby, http://www.tcj.com/jack-kirby-interview/

127 Kristin Thomson, *Reflections on Cars*, http://www.davidbordwell.net/blog/2006/10/08/reflections-on-cars/

128 *The Oxford Companion to United States History*, Oxford University Press, 2001, p.678

129 Norman Klein, *7 Minutes: The Life and Death of the American Cartoon*, Verso Books, 1995

130 Philip French review of *Cars* in *The Observer*, http://www.guardian.co.uk/film/movie/113137/cars

131 Roger Ebert review of *Cars* in the *Chicago Sun Times*, http://rogerebert.suntimes.com/apps/pbcs.dll/article?AID=/20060608/REVIEWS/60606002

132 *Empire* review of *Cars*, http://www.empireonline.com/reviews/review.asp?FID=9827

133 Don Bluth interviewed by Bob Thomas, *The Evening News*, 4 January 1987, http://news.google.com/newspapers?nid=1696&dat=19861217&id=uC4bAAAAIBAJ&sjid=BkkEAAAAIBAJ&pg=5857,5535271

134 Harley Jessup interviewed by Ron Barbagallo, http://animationartconservation.com/?c=art&p=articles_ratatouille

135 Michael Giacchino, www.Usatoday.com/life/movies/movieawards/Oscars/2008-02-18-oscar-newcomer-giacchinoN.htm

136 Roger Ebert, review of *Ratatouille*, http://rogerebert.suntimes.com/apps/pbcs.dll/article?AID=/20070830/REVIEWS/708300303

137 Philip French, review of *Ratatouille*, http://www.guardian.co.uk/film/movie/119669/ratatouille

138 Peter Hartlaub, review of *Ratatouille*, http://www.sfgate.com/movies/article/Ooh-la-la-A-rat-cooks-up-a-masterpiece-2554473.php

139 *The Oxford Companion to Fairy Tales*, Edited by Jack Zipes, Oxford University Press, 2002, p.xxv

140 Robert Bresson, quoted by Paul Schrader, *Transcendental Style in Film: Ozu, Bresson and Dreyer*, DaCapo Press, 1988, p.65

141 Walter Murch, *Sound Design: The Dancing Shadow in Projections 4*, edited by John Boorman, Tom Luddy, David Thomson and Walter Donohue, Faber and Faber, 1995, p.239

142 Ben Burtt – www.moviesonline.ca/movienews_14930.html

143 J P Telotte, *Human Artifice and the Science Fiction Film*, *Film Quarterly*, Vol. 36, no. 3 (Spring 1983), p.180

144 Ralph Eggleston interviewed by Ron Barbagallo, *Design With A Purpose: An Interview with Ralph Eggleston*, Animation Art Conservation, http://animationartconservation.com/?c=art&p=articles_content

145 Andrew Stanton, http://www.cinemablend.com/new/Interview-WALL-E-s-Andrew-Stanton-9323.html

146 Roger Ebert, review of *Wall-E*, http://www.rogerebert.com/reviews/wall-e-2008

147 Olly Richards review of *Wall E*, http://www.empireonline.com/reviews/reviewcomplete.asp?FID=134838

148 Bill Plympton, www.kickstarter.com/projects

149 Harold Bloom, *The Knight in the Mirror*, *Guardian*, 13 December 2003, http://www.guardian.co.uk/books/2003/dec/13/classics.miguelcervantes

150 Michael Giacchino discussing the score for *Up*, http://www.youtube.com/watch?v=vACcAdCjIzk

151 Jim Kitses quoted by James Clarke in *What inspiration blooms, watered by stormy weather*, Times Higher Education Magazine, 6 August 2012, http://www.timeshighereducation.co.uk/features/culture/what-inspiration-blooms-watered-by-stormy-weather/420803.article

152 Michael Chabon, *Manhood for Amateurs: The Wilderness of Childhood*, in The New York Review of Books, 16 July 2009, http://www.nybooks.com/articles/archives/2009/jul/16/manhood-for-amateurs-the-wilderness-of-childhood/?pagination=false

153 Roger Ebert review of *Up*, http://www.rogerebert.com/reviews/up-2009

154 Dave Calhoun review of *Up*, *Time Out*, http://www.timeout.com/film/reviews/86732/up.html

155 Ian Freer review of *Up* in *Empire*, http://www.empireonline.com/reviews/review.asp?FID=135479

156 Alison Lurie, *Boys and Girls Forever*, Vintage Books, 2004

157 Ibid

158 Ibid

159 Mark Twain, Chapter: *Nothing More to Write*, The Adventures of Huckleberry Finn, The Portable Mark Twain, Penguin Books, 1987, p.539

160 Gaston Bachelard, *The Poetics of Space*, Beacon Press, 1992, p.6

The Films of Pixar Animation Studio

161 Lee Unkrich, quoted by Mark Lee, interview with Lee Unkrich about *Toy Story 3*, www.telegraph.co.uk, http://www.telegraph.co.uk/culture/film/filmmakersonfilm/7879992/Toy-Story-3-interview-with-director-Lee-Unkrich.html

162 Ibid

163 Michael Arndt interview, www.blogsindiewire.com/thompsononhollywood/michaelarndt

164 Michael Arndt interview, www.animatedviews.com/2010/toy-story-3

165 Maureen Furniss, *Art in Motion: Animation Aesthetics*, Revised Edition, John Libbey Books, 2008

166 John Canemaker, quoted by Amid Amidi, www.cartoonbrew.com, 12 July 2010, http://www.cartoonbrew.com/books/interview-with-john-canemaker-about-two-guys-named-joe-25219.html

167 Roger Ebert, review of *Toy Story 3*, http://www.rogerebert.com/reviews/toy-story-3-2010

168 Dan Jolin review of *Toy Story 3*, *Empire* magazine, http://www.empireonline.com/reviews/reviewcomplete.asp?FID=135545

169 Ben Queen interview with *Animated Views*, www.animatedviews.com /2011/cars-2-screenwriter-ben-queen-on-the-race-for-his-art-of-book/

170 John Lasseter, quoted by Alex Dorn, *John Lasseter on Cars 2, story, and the future of shorts at Pixar*, http://www.hitfix.com/blogs/motion-captured/posts/john-lasseter-on-cars-2-story-and-the-future-of-shorts-at-pixar

171 Patrick Goldstein, *Oscars 2012: Is Pixar's Animation Winning Streak Over?*, *Los Angeles Times*, 9 November 2011, movies.about.com/od/cars2

172 Roger Ebert review of *Cars 2*, http://www.rogerebert.com/reviews/cars-2-2011

173 Ian Freer review of *Cars 2*, *Empire*, http://www.empireonline.com/reviews/review.asp?FID=135549

174 Brenda Chapman quoted by Nicole Sperling, *When The Glass Ceiling Crashed on Brenda Chapman*, *Los Angeles Times*, 25 May 2011, http://articles.latimes.com/2011/may/25/entertainment/la-et-women-animation-sidebar-20110525

175 http://www.slate.com/articles/arts/movies/2013/06/monsters_university_the_monsters_inc_prequel_reviewed.html

176 http://www.bleedingcool.com/2012/06/05/john-lasseter-explains-pixars-the-good-dinosaur-and-pete-docters-inside-the-mind-movie/

177 Thomas G Smith, *Industrial Light and Magic: The Art of Visual Effects*, Columbus Books, 1986

178 14 February 2012, Cartoonbrew intvw. with Enrico Casarosa, http://www.cartoonbrew.com/cgi/oscar-focus-enrico-casarosa-on-la-luna-56410.html

188

INDEX